The
Restful
Mind

His Eminence Gyalwa Dokhampa

The Restful Mind

A New Way of Thinking
A New Way of Life

His Eminence Gyalwa Dokhampa

yellow
kite

First published in Great Britain in 2013 by Hodder & Stoughton
An Hachette UK company

First published in paperback in 2018 by Yellow Kite
An imprint of Hodder & Stoughton

1

ISBN 978 1 444 76231 0

Printed and bound by CPI Group (UK) Ltd, Croydon, CR0 4YY

Hodder & Stoughton policy is to use papers that are natural,
renewable and recyclable products and made from wood grown in
sustainable forests. The logging and manufacturing processes are expected
to conform to the environmental regulations of the country of origin.

Yellow Kite
Hodder & Stoughton Ltd
Carmelite House,
50 Victoria Embankment
London EC4Y 0DZ

www.yellowkitebooks.co.uk
www.hodder.co.uk

I dedicate this book to his Holiness the present Gyalwang Drukpa, by whose grace I have developed the confidence to understand that the source of all happiness and pain is none other than one's own mind.

Contents

About the Author

His Eminence the Gyalwa Dokhampa, more popularly known as 'Khamtrul Rinpoche', teaches worldwide bringing a young and vibrant viewpoint to traditional Buddhist teachings. Since 2000, he has shared his knowledge and warmth of personality with students in the USA, Europe, Mexico, Bhutan, Vietnam, Malaysia, Hong Kong, Taiwan, Singapore and Peru, he has led annual retreats in Nepal and Bhutan, and been a keynote speaker at the Buddhism and Science Symposium – 'Growing a Beautiful Mind' – in Singapore.

The Gyalwa Dokhampa emphasises that Buddhism is not a religion, but rather a way to finding happiness. He also works to make Buddhist ideals relevant to a modern lifestyle, so that they may be integrated into everyday life, less through self-help than through self-lessness and generosity to others: as we give to others, we give to ourselves.

His Eminence the Gyalwa Dokhampa Jigme Pema Nyinjadh was born in 1981, into the family of His Holiness the Gyalwang Drukpa, supreme head of the Drukpa Lineage, and was recognised by His Holiness the Dalai Lama as the ninth incarnation of the Gyalwa Dokhampa. He studied at Druk Thupten Sangag Choeling Monastery in Darjeeling, where he spent his childhood and teenage years under the guidance of his principal teacher, His Holiness the Gyalwang Drukpa. Later he completed a nine-year course to attain his Master's degree in Buddhist Philosophy from Tango Monastic University, Royal Kingdom of Bhutan. He is now continuing the secret inner practices of the Vajrayana from both His Holiness the Gyalwang Drukpa and His Holiness Je Thrizur Tenzin Dhodup (the 68th Je-Khenpo of Bhutan).

www.facebook.com/Gyalwa.Dokhampa.Khamtrul
www.gyalwadokhampa.org
@GyalwaDokhampa

Introduction

It is with our minds that we create our world and our place within it: all the experiences that we go through – of happiness, sadness, suffering, beauty, anything – are given meaning and come to life in our mind. So understanding how your mind works, I believe, is the key to freedom, to happiness, to contentment and to overcoming challenges. It is the key to everything.

None of us can stop the continuum of life; as much as we might wish to, we can't stop time. We can't prevent ourselves from eventually getting old, and none of us knows when we will die, only that it is inevitable. Now you may think I am being pessimistic, but I am really only pointing out that what we so often end up dwelling on in our minds are the things we can't change, like time passing, rather than those we can, like *how* we live our lives. This is the part we get to choose, so why not train our minds a little better to focus on this opportunity? Why not teach our minds to grab life with both hands and get straight to the good stuff? And why not allow and encourage ourselves to let go of the many expectations and fears that end up ruling our thoughts and, in turn, our actions.

The meaning in our life comes from our efforts to benefit others, in whatever way we are able, day to day. Yet it is all too easy nowadays to get carried away with the many things going on in our minds: worries about the future, looking over the fence at what our neighbours have, our ever-growing to-do lists. Such thinking builds a wall between ourselves and our inner nature – the part deep within that knows our path, who we are and our place in the world. We need to break down that barrier and reconnect with the restful mind that has always been within because it is our essence. Then we can go ahead and live with confidence and freedom.

When asked then, what is my personal message, I would say I have two; one is from a Buddhist perspective and the other is from a psychological perspective. The only difference really is one of language.

The key is that I hope to remind people that they can change their lives through a balance of two things: what goes on in their minds and how they act on their thoughts. So it's really a combination of being and then doing, each in turn positively affecting the other. It is with our minds that we put the meaning into what we do each day, and then with our mindful actions that we can contribute to the conditions for our own happiness and that of others. If, therefore, we ever discover that we are not feeling happy in our day-to-day life, instead of looking outside of ourselves for the cause, we learn to look within for understanding, to turn a light on appreciating everything we do have, rather than always looking for what is missing. We need to understand that our restful mind depends on no one but ourselves, and when we begin to understand that we are our own master – our own Buddha, as we say in Buddhist philosophy – then we can take care of our minds, infusing life with more joy, more positive action and more peace. And even if enlightenment is still quite far away, we will certainly feel less messed up.

The Restless Mind

Sometimes in life we feel restless, and that however hard we try we don't know our own mind. Our thoughts seem to take on a life of their own, rushing headlong from one experience or emotion to the next, always looking for something, although quite what we might not even know. Even the thought of slowing down makes us anxious – what will we achieve then? We ask ourselves so many questions and are no longer sure of the answers. We set our sights on something or someone and then, somewhere along the way, we forget that while we started the whole journey to be happy, happiness came fleetingly and then fell by the wayside. So we become agitated and feel an urge to move on to the next thing, to grab another bit of happiness, or success, or just do things differently, because we can't be sure that what we have now is ever enough.

In our day-to-day lives our minds are constantly stimulated by communication, virtual connection. Information overload. Choice overload. The opportunities to learn, to create and to be inspired, surround us, but leave little or no space in which our minds can actually stretch and grow. We're asking many questions, yet we haven't the time or patience to sit for a moment to hear or understand the answers. And we spend so much time running around searching for solutions that we forget to look directly into the true nature of the problem. Sometimes, or even most of the time, our minds feel a bit like a pinball machine, always shooting off at angles, all over the place. If only we could feel settled in our minds and happy with where we are and the direction in which we're facing. If only our minds could stop overcomplicating, overanalysing, *overthinking*.

One of my teachers put it well: 'Man – because he sacrifices his health in order to make money, then sacrifices his money to recuperate his health, then is so anxious about the future that he doesn't enjoy the present and, as a result, he doesn't live in the present or the future – lives as if he's never going to die and then dies having never really lived.' It is a pattern that's easy to fall into. Happiness is always around the next corner, and even when we find it, sometimes we have forgotten what we were looking for in the first place. We wear our busyness like a badge of honour, even though we know deep down that the number of things we get done in the day do not equate to happiness and contentment, or even achievement. As we fill our days, and our minds, we might sometimes feel as though we are living life according to some kind of script, not written by ourselves: rushing here and there, never feeling we have spent quite enough time with people or tasks, spreading ourselves too thin.

We might gradually find that it's more difficult to make decisions, as we become hesitant or fearful of getting things 'wrong'. Or we stop celebrating in the efforts of others, instead comparing ourselves and constantly competing. We're so busy, but we're finding it hard to get any one thing done well. There is a feeling of unease; we might not sleep so well, or we might sleep so much that we feel sluggish and heavy. We lose touch with good friends, our family annoy us and our boss is a nightmare. Time is slipping by.

The restless mind is frightened of the quiet; it is easily bored – busy, busy, busy. The restless mind overthinks every minute detail and decision of life, often fearful, anxious or just unable to stop: what if I had done that differently? What if I get it wrong? What if they don't like me? Why did they say that? Am I good enough? Are they good enough? What am I going to do once I've done the washing up? And after that, and after that . . . In the restless mind the imagination runs wild, yet rarely creatively. Life goes by in a blur, while often at the same time feeling stuck; we constantly crave company, while feeling lonely in the crowd.

Now remember when your mind was restful.

The restful mind is playful, creative and alert. Enjoyment comes easily. Sadness comes easily too, but is no longer crippling. The restful mind is understanding. With a restful mind we give ourselves and others a break and see the good. The restful mind is relaxed and confident without a need for arrogance. There is time to care, time to inspire, to be inspired and get so much done. Watch the child who has a completely natural, restful mind. They are curious and observant, but also still, entranced by the moment. They are right there completely at one with the present.

I like to talk and teach about the restful mind because when we give ourselves a chance to calm and nourish our mind, then we open up the time and space for understanding to come; understanding of our true nature and that of others. We can get back in touch. Understanding is the essence of everything – it is there in all of us, completely naturally, but often we become unbalanced, only listening to what's happening on the surface of our mind. You can almost physically feel this: your energy is buzzing in your head without being grounded in the understanding of your heart or your gut – your inner mind.

A restful mind is far from lazy, it is a mind of action.

It can get so much more done, be quick and nimble, light on its feet, make decisions easily with all senses involved and with a good heart. But without understanding we can easily get caught up in the fabrications of our minds – a constant stream of expectations, worries, projections, labels, preconceptions and judgements. It's exhausting, to the extent that even our sleep feels disrupted by our wild mind.

The restful mind is open, rather than narrow. There is space to consider things from different angles, space to let things just be. We become more considerate of others. We notice more. We have time to listen and to smile. We invite and attract good things, like a smile from another, kindness, knowledge.

I hope that as we go through these pages together the wonderful nature of your own mind will begin to become clearer. Of course, it's not all calm and perfect; life is so interesting precisely because it is full of ups and downs, challenges and excitement. You might even think at first that it's boring to approach such things with a restful mind. Surely some things in life deserve more drama and extreme reactions? I'm not here to convince you; it's completely up to you. But I hope as you discover your own nature, beneath all the layers of self-labelling and ego, expectations and attachments, that you'll see for yourself how energising it can be to appreciate without clinging, how something like patience can free you up from so many pointless judgements, how you don't have to find a solution for every problem, but that you can create a fertile ground for ideas, making decisions, planting the seeds of great actions and so much more.

This book may provide something of a 'retreat' for you and your mind. Retreats are popular in the Buddhist tradition because they give us a quiet and focused space in which to learn and explore the teachings – to practise putting things into practice! But we always say that the teachings are meaningless if we can *only* practise them on retreat. Bringing them into everyday life is the true practice. If you can bring the restful mind to a busy city life, for example, then that is something special in this modern world. It shows that it is possible to make even the smallest space feel wide and limitless, and that even a great many obstacles that might come along during your day can be dissolved with a restful mind.

In Tibetan, the word for 'retreat' means 'boundary', and so it is that when we go on a mind retreat we explore how our mind and emotions work and where our boundaries lie between good and happy emotions and afflictive ones. These boundaries do not have to restrict us. Awareness gives us great freedom. We begin to realise how a given external situation can be approached from different angles. We can observe things like anger and see where it comes from, and whether it ever truly helps. We stop trying to fix things in certainty; we stop trying so hard to change others. We relax.

In this way I like to think of training the mind from

the depths of the heart, bringing the two together as one.

We will also explore the relationship between body and mind. We can learn so much about our emotions through the signs our body gives us. It will often tell us before the mind when we are about to overstep our healthy emotional boundaries. We can feel anger or embarrassment coming as our inner thermometer rises. We can hear how alien and strained our voice often sounds when on the defensive. We can use our mind to help calm our body, and use our body to calm our mind, especially through the breath. We can connect with nature through our feet as we walk, which, in turn, helps us connect with our own inner nature. I think it is no coincidence that good diet and exercise are so often prescribed for mild depression or anxiety. Our healthy body can do much to help our inner mindfulness, bringing both into balance.

A Little Contemplation Goes a Long Way

Meditation is a simple practice we use to help us understand our world and to watch ourselves. It brings us back into ourselves, calming the surface, so that we might have a look at what's going on beneath. It might at first seem like a very selfish practice, to spend time gazing inwards, rather than focusing on others (in fact, interestingly, the word Buddhist means 'insider'), but it is only by checking in on ourselves that we begin to truly appreciate and respect others. It is only by opening up that we can see what we need to repair and restore, face our arrogance and change the frequency of our mind. It stops us becoming complacent. It is easy to spend a lifetime pointing at others and saying what's good or bad about them, but of course we're always looking through our own lens, with our own agenda. Through contemplation our self-awareness grows and we can admit that the faults we see in others are often our own. Likewise, we can learn to live and let live more and genuinely celebrate in the efforts of others. Just think how it feels to be jealous of a co-worker, compared with the feeling of sincerely congratulating another's efforts or successes, of being happy for them.

If we give ourselves just a little time, even a few minutes daily, for quiet and contemplation, then we soon become more observant throughout our day, more appreciative of the moment and more focused on the task at hand, rather than worrying about the next one. I find that meditation is very uplifting and really helps to develop a sense of happiness, so that rather than being something which happens to or is given to us, it becomes a feeling we nourish and nurture from within.

Understanding the Nature of the Mind

Without understanding, knowledge and practice are often of little use. All three are interdependent. It's like any change in life: if we don't really get why we want to make the change, then it's never likely to last. If we don't prepare ourselves, it's unlikely to endure. And if we don't jump in at some point and give it a go, then we don't even give ourselves a chance.

So we start, in Part One, by gaining some understanding of the mind and, in particular, the conceptual or 'dualistic' mind. This is how we most often see and interpret the world. Everything is given a label through our own particular lens – either 'good' or 'bad' – and while this might change from moment to moment, it sets us up to be constantly comparing and judging. From 'Am I good or bad', to 'Is that flower beautiful or ugly?' we are always questioning, constantly making assertions. It's completely understandable that we do this, as we try to make sense of the world, but it also tends to set us up for frustration and disappointment. Our concepts define but then divide us, limiting us so that there is no space to stretch out in the sun and grow.

We will explore the tendency to look externally for our emotions, for the source of and solutions to our problems; using both modern science and modern Buddhism, which rather wonderfully use different language to say the same thing. We will look directly into the nature of happiness, anger, loneliness, desire. We will face our worries and our fears. To do this we turn the camera inwards. We re-introduce ourselves to our own minds, while engaging our heart and our compassion at the same time, and begin to just look, replacing constant analysis with awareness.

This is when we begin to notice our 'ego mind': the mind that is always clamouring for our attention, and also our inner nature, or our restful mind, often getting on with things much more quietly and happily beneath the bluster of the ego. As we watch, we become more aware of the differences between the two. Our ego demands instant, often emotional reactions, while the restful mind goes at a more gentle pace, yet seems so often to be the one to keep us on track when we give it a chance to shine. Sometimes we lack the confidence to listen to our quiet mind, and doubt ourselves.

We might become a bit fearful or indecisive, getting stuck in negative patterns, or constantly moving on, sure that must somehow be the answer. And yet the nagging feeling is still there – our inner nature waiting patiently for us to have courage and turn the spotlight inwards, find our true purpose and share that with the world.

The Mind Retreat

The second part of this book is the Mind Retreat. You can learn the tools of the restful mind wherever you happen to be, and while you don't need to go up a mountain (although it does so happen that going to a high place for meditation allows you to see the world better), I would encourage you to give yourself some time and space at this point.

It is important that whenever we decide to make a change in life we commit all our energy to seeing it through. The tools of breathing, meditation, contemplation and mindfulness are not complicated, but can really change our general state of mind and so have a beneficial effect on both daily life and how we see the bigger picture. The key message here is one of 'practice', because like any skill in life, the restful mind benefits most from a little practice every day. Just a few minutes are all that's needed, but a big effort may still be required to fit those minutes into the day at first, in order that they become a habit. This is why we need to develop a little understanding first, as this provides the motivation needed to commit to changing or training the mind.

Bringing calm to the stressed mind is the first effect of the simple techniques we learn, and if you were to go no further than that you will feel an opening up in your mind over a very short period of time as you teach your body and mind how to relax. You will see the difference this brings to daily life, as you let go of old thought patterns and allow lots more space for things like patience, compromise and flexibility, because a relaxed and restful mind is an open mind.

By simply looking at life with appreciation, just shining a light on and saying thank you for anything or anyone that is good, we discover so much more room for others and our capacity for patience and tolerance, and happiness, grows. It doesn't mean denying or covering up the less good things, but just for a few moments focusing on the positive. When we don't think about them on a daily basis we tend to forget the good things in life, so taking a few minutes to focus on what we do have, rather than what we don't is a powerful exercise that can infuse our whole day with a different feel.

A core aspect of the restful mind is to understand and accept the constantly changing nature of life; to be accepting of the things we can't control, rather than worrying about them so much or getting angry with them. We learn to stop looking outside of ourselves for the things we think we need to make us happy and begin to realise that it is how we see the world, *how we think* that determines our happiness and contentment. So it is our reactions to situations that really matter, not the situations themselves, which are so often beyond our control.

We also practise bringing ourselves back into the present: the past is past and the future uncertain. What we have is today, and being more mindful of the moment helps to get away from all the usual what-ifs that constantly play out in our imaginations. We reconnect with ourselves, with the people around us and with our world, and instead of letting our thoughts and emotions run wild, worrying about tomorrow, we are alert and aware today and more mindful of our words and actions, rather than constantly judging those of others.

Another tool of the restful mind is getting to know ourselves better, while realising at the same time that the world doesn't revolve around 'me'. It is good to know that we are all special, but also not very special at all! So don't think it is selfish to spend time getting to know who we have become, because especially in today's modern world many layers have built up over time, distancing us from our inner nature, the part of us who simply wants to be happy and give happiness too. It is good to turn the flashlight on our own minds and try to peel back some of those layers – maybe even letting some of them go.

In fact, much of the mind retreat is about letting go – whether that is letting go of particular ways of seeing and thinking that have built up over time, of our attitudes or our pride, of thinking we know so much, letting go of fears, grief or letting go of the negative influences in our lives. This doesn't mean that you will no longer feel emotions like anger, grief, jealousy or frustration, but when you are disturbed by such emotions you will be able to gently investigate and ask yourself why these emotions have arisen, and so more easily move on.

We also look to restore the healthy body to help the restful mind. Sometimes, it is a good idea to take time off from our minds through exercising the body, or equally we can use activities like walking or eating to calm and focus the mind.

Everyday Mindfulness

In Part Three we bring the restful mind into the everyday. It's all well and good being calm and collected when we're walking along the seashore, but how about when a stranger is shouting at us from their car or our boss is disappointed in our work? How can we use all of our senses and listen to our inner voice when making decisions? What about the days when we just feel life is getting on top of us, when we feel bored or are so busy we can't think what to do next. What about when old feelings of somehow not being good enough creep up? And what about the catastrophic times or events in our lives – when grief threatens to overwhelm us or when we are facing illness or harm? The answers are within us, but we all need help with finding the way. We are all beginners.

Mindfulness has its roots in Buddhism, although modern science is rapidly catching up on this ancient way of living. There are now wonderful programmes which teach mindfulness, which has already been shown to help with depression to the same degree as medication. I hope that us Buddhists may be of a little help on this journey too. We are not scientists, but to us, mindfulness is simply being in your life, in the everyday. My teacher His Holiness Gyalwang Drukpa was recently asked about mindfulness and he said that one of the best moments is just before you go to sleep, as you are dropping off. As we know from our teachings and our experiences, if you are mindful, ie. relaxed and calm in that moment between being awake and asleep, you will have eight hours or so of mindful sleep. It turns out that sleep experts too have determined that our minds actually help us to process our day and any unresolved thoughts during sleep. So it makes sense to go to sleep in a good frame of mind, in order to benefit from a very helpful, restful and refreshing night's sleep.

Lots of people ask: if we become so caught up with noticing every tiny detail in life, where will our spontaneity – our passion – go? For me, mindfulness goes hand in hand with spontaneity because we notice opportunities in the moment, staring us in the face, rather than keeping our heads down. Mindfulness is about letting your mind go free, letting go of all the shoulds, ifs, buts and maybes. What would you do today if you had no fear?

I can't offer you instant fixes for all of the challenges you will come across during your lifetime; I can't offer a soundbite that you can repeat over and over to calm your rush-hour anxiety or allay your worries about work. But what I hope I can do is encourage you in a new way of thinking that will, with practice, help with all of these situations. I am offering you a set of tools for the mind that will gradually develop into a way of thinking and a way of seeing the world that is no longer at odds, either with yourself or others, but one that embraces the potential of life. These tools will act as reminders, grounding you while also setting your mind free.

We are our thoughts, words and actions. That is why caring for our minds is so important as our thoughts are the beginning of the chain reaction that leads to our words and, ultimately, our actions. It is with the mind that we create our world and how we're going to live in it. So open up and let the world in.

1

The Nature of the Mind

If a man does not keep pace with his companions,
perhaps it is because he hears a different drummer. Let
him step to the music which he hears, however
measured or far away.
Henry David Thoreau

Why do we do what we do, and what is it that stops us from following our dreams? This question is at the heart of this book, and at the heart of what brings restlessness into the mind. And when we begin to explore the answers, we see that it is also at the heart of the restful mind.

Why do we do what we do? Such a simple question and yet when the busyness of life takes over it becomes clouded by so many external factors. When we start out in life we do what we do to be fed and loved, to be happy and make others happy too: we gurgle and laugh, our parents are delighted and beam back at us, so we gurgle and laugh a bit more. We play the games that interest us, are fearless and voracious in our learning. We don't pre-judge, we just live each day for the day, for the amazing things will we see next.

As we grow up, we begin to think more about what it is in our studies or in life that fascinates us, or that we happen to be good at. We hone our skills and expertise. The sky is the limit when we start out. And the heart of 'why we do what we do' is very strong:

- to have and give happiness in some way
- to provide for ourselves and others
- to take care of people
- to take care of the earth
- to make a difference.

Most, if not all of us are driven to have a good life. And depending on who we are as individuals, that can encompass all manner of things: we may hope to care for others in some way, to inform others or entertain them; we may get caught up in thinking we do what we do for the trappings in life, for a bigger car or house, but even then, deep down, there is still something that gives us reason within. We may not be able to explain why we are even here, but we know that we have some degree of control, to a lesser or greater extent, over who we are going to be in this life.

So why do we so often find that we aren't actually getting on with the life we want, the life that is important? What are the things that keep stopping us? We might think it is other people, or circumstances beyond our control – that it's not something we can do anything about, or that we have personal responsibilities that mean we can't just drop a good job that we drag ourselves to every day in order to follow our dreams.

Why do we procrastinate about so many things? We manage to identify something good that we want to do and then keep putting it off, making our minds even more restless as now we feel bad that we can't seem to just get on with it. It feels like we are sabotaging ourselves. We know that when we are in the flow of getting on with something we feel happy and content, revitalised and really engaged. Yet we also find it very easy to put our mental energy in the wrong place, often focusing outwards on the very things that we can't change, rather than looking inwards at what we can.

We need to remind ourselves why we do what we do, to get back in touch with our nature, find strength, inspiration and know that while we can't always change what is outside of us, we can do something about what is within.

This is when we begin to really explore the nature of our mind and our heart, to understand the perceptions, fears and worries that have built up over time and are now limiting and restricting us. Perhaps we think we are a certain type of person, that our faults and weaknesses are a part of our DNA. We forget that those very weaknesses might also be a source of great strength (which we will explore later in the book). We let fear creep in and when we don't remember to keep looking it in the face, we turn around one day to discover it has been stopping us from doing all sorts of great things. We find ourselves constantly comparing ourselves to others, looking over to see who has more, somehow thinking that happiness will go to those who are more successful or more attractive.

And then something happens that stops the world for a moment and reminds us why we do what we do. This is the seed that is nourished and cared for by the restful mind, the mind where we know and accept ourselves and others more readily, with less judgement, more openness and with compassion. A moment with our child reminds us why we are a parent, why we care so deeply for others. An hour spent completely focused on a task, caught up in the flow, reminds us why we learn skills or want to develop our creativity. Suddenly, we can't think why we always seem to procrastinate so much, or why we get so worked up over unimportant things. By getting to know our minds better the aim is to shine a light on both why it can feel rushed or wild, fearful and claustrophobic, and also how to bring us closer to what lies beneath the bluster and the waves, to the source of our true sense of happiness, peace and contentment.

Three Things to Help You Get Started

On my travels, I find that many people are interested in listening because they are looking for ways to get over the stress in their lives, be it in their job, relationship or just within their mind. They want to be able to calm their mind. The first step is often to see how things like meditation or mindfulness can help in day-to-day life. And once they begin to see this, they often want to go a little further and really begin to explore the mind, to understand themselves and those around them.

Whenever I begin to teach, I focus on three things which I think are important to understand so that you can see how all of this living philosophy can benefit you in your life.

The first is that *no being or thing has the ability to completely take away your suffering.* The only person who can do this is you. A very compassionate friend or loved one, even a kind stranger, may help to create the conditions for you to let go of your suffering, but ultimately it is down to you. This might sound negative at first, but it is actually very encouraging because it means that we have a big part to play in whatever difficulties and whatever good things we are going through. Our ways of thinking, how we act and how we look at situations affect the kind of experiences we go through. For example, if two people are going through the same difficulty, like losing a job, but they have different outlooks, one may suffer a lot, while the other feels the pain a little less and even looks for the silver lining. So while one person may be very attached to his or her fame or wealth, suffering greatly at its loss, another who understands that by nature such things are impermanent, and who therefore feels less attached to them, may suffer less at the loss. You can begin to see how our perceptions can play a part in our happiness or suffering.

The second thing is that *everything is interdependent*. When things happen, they are never caused by just one condition – they are the result of many conditions coming together, both external and internal. So an external condition might be that our partner leaves us, but our level of suffering also relies on how we react internally to such an external condition and the part we played in the collapse of the relationship, because there is never only one good side and one bad. Think about how we can seem to love and then sometimes be very unhappy with the same person; our feelings towards them might go up and down like a rollercoaster because there are so many other factors at play. Ironically, we often spend a great deal of time and effort trying to control our external conditions, while letting our internal reactions run wild. When we understand this concept of interdependence, then we see that we are not totally helpless. This is not to deny the strength of those external conditions, but just to demonstrate that there is always a degree of choice when it comes to our own thoughts and reactions.

Think about the suffering we cause ourselves internally through getting angry or jealous. Say that another person shouts abuse at us: we can become very angry and upset or we can keep calm and deal with the situation without becoming attached to our own emotions about it. This isn't about never being angry or upset, but about how much we hold on to such restless emotions.

The third point that I like to introduce is the idea that *nothing exists as it appears to be.* This isn't always a very easy concept, but if we stay with the examples of happiness and suffering, then it is realising that these are not concrete 'things', but very much a reflection of one's perception. And the same is true for such emotions as anger, or what we see as beauty, what is good. If you ask ten people about their idea of happiness, they will all have different ideas, from money or love to peace and quiet. When you begin to understand how changeable happiness or suffering is, then you rely less on external conditions. You may appreciate that you have a nice job and earn good money, but become less dependent on these for your inner happiness. You know that today or tomorrow things may change, and that's ok, because you are still you. Similarly, you begin to understand that you are not anger, you are not jealousy or sadness – these are simply states of mind that come and go, rather than being fixed in existence. So if that's the case, we realise we can change our own minds and even train our minds, whatever our situation might be.

So:

1. Our happiness or suffering comes from within
2. We can't control the things or people that are external to us, that happen to us, but we can control our own reactions or way of looking at things, so we need never be completely helpless
3. Nothing is set in stone, especially our minds

These three points of understanding are the beginning: they are the essence of the teachings that we can apply to our daily lives and thinking.

Let's take an example to show what I mean. Something that makes a great many people feel restless in their minds in the modern world is travel – from the fear of getting on a plane to waiting everyday at the bus stop, never sure when the next bus will come, or being pushed out of the way by determined, even rude, commuters at the height of rush hour. You wonder why you put yourself through it, feeling helpless that you have no choice if you want to get to work on time or have that wonderful holiday your partner has set their heart on. You feel like you waste so much time, unable even to read as you stand squashed on a train. Why can't that pushy person just be nice? Why do people have to be so rude, looking down into their newspapers, rather than standing up for the pregnant woman?

So how do the 'three things' help in a frustrating situation like the daily rush-hour commute? What can they really do, in practice, to calm our minds down and make us feel better?

Feelings of helplessness can make you feel you don't really have control over your emotions, and that it is only external factors that are running the show in your mind. But the reality is that whatever is going on around you, you do have a choice as to how you are going to react. You can take matters into your own hands on a practical level to help your mind, and decide to leave for work fifteen minutes earlier, taking some of the tension out of your journey. That way you feel calmer knowing that you won't have to rush and so you may be less quick to react strongly to those people pushing and shoving.

But there are always more factors at play than just one in any situation. So while there might be a few people who look down into their books, rather than up to check if anyone might need their seat, there are just as many who will readily give up theirs with a smile, and the exchange of goodwill when this happens is really heart-warming on a cramped commute home. You might be that kind person and get a lovely surprised smile in return.

Also, however tied you might be to arriving or leaving work at a specific time, for example, your mind is not tied to a particular way of spending that time in your imagination. So instead of spending so much mental energy on feeling annoyed and finding people to dislike, you might contemplate the good things that have happened recently, write a love letter in your mind or simply focus on your breathing to relax your body. You might lose yourself in a great book, and sometimes just be, letting your mind settle and clear in preparation for your day.

Later in the book there are specific ways to help you feel calmer during stressful moments, particularly through focusing on the breath. But at the heart of all the teachings here are these three things and how we can always remind ourselves that it is with our own minds that we create our own world. Reality isn't a fixed thing; it is created through our perceptions and our beliefs. It is up to us how we look at the things in our lives, the great things and the difficult things. Happiness is something for which we can sow the seed ourselves, and that we can nurture, grow and share with others through our love, kindness and generosity. It's easy with the busyness and pressures of life to fall out of the habit of happiness – to begin to feel out of sorts or to let negative thoughts and emotions take hold – but with just a little understanding and practice we can get back into the happiness habit, whatever situations life may bring us.

My own spiritual teacher, His Holiness Gyalwang Drukpa, has a simple saying that I think goes to the heart of this point: 'If today went well, then great. If it didn't go so well, that's ok too.' By being a little more comfortable with uncertainty and at ease with the ups and downs of life, we bring less of a sense of struggle into our lives. We accept that there are many things which are beyond our control, but that how we respond and react within ourselves is always our choice.

What do you need to know about your mind to make your life better?

Before any change for the better can take place, a level of understanding is always needed; if we never take the time to study our minds we tend to fall back on the automatic responses and reactions that we have built up over our lives. We don't even know we're doing it, but at the first hint of trouble we retreat to what we know, or rather what our subconscious thinks we know.

Such automatic responses of the mind are in the main actually very helpful to us. We don't have to relearn every day how to drive a car or even put one foot in front of the other. We don't have to weigh up the pros and cons of each and every choice we make in the day, but can just go ahead and have porridge or granola without worrying too much about it.

The problem is that if we stay in autopilot too much, then we are really restricting our potential. We might be able to get through the day in one piece but we know somehow that we are limiting our own wisdom and not opening ourselves up to what life truly has to offer. We might feel that we are stuck in those automatic habits for too much of our day, and that some of them have become negative, rather than helpful (for example, the daily glass of wine that signals the end of the work day).

Science has really been getting into the mind, trying to see just how it all works, why chronic conditions of the mind such as stress, anxiety and depression are affecting more and more people and what we can do to try and look after our minds. Much has been written about recently of the two aspects of the mind. Conscious and unconscious, slow thinking and fast thinking, the lizard brain, the chimp. Although Buddhist philosophy has also talked of two states of mind for thousands of years, which you might call the 'outer ego' and 'inner nature', we are very much beginners in this field, but we can, I hope, offer a language of the mind that may be complementary to the science. I think perhaps we also offer the possibility of another dimension: beneath the layers of the conscious and unconscious mind and beyond all this thinking – that of our inner nature, our heart.

Taming the elephant

Thousands of years ago Buddha compared training the mind to taming a wild elephant because properly trained wild elephants have the capacity to be of great help, while wild elephants can be extremely distractive.

The emotional, often unconscious part of our mind may be compared to the wild elephant, whereas we also have a cognitive part of the brain which is conscious, rational and usually focused towards the outside world. In the modern world, a balance between these two parts of the brain, a balance within our mind, is key to looking after ourselves, turning restless into restful, discomfort into peace. Both parts have much to offer us. If we don't tame the elephant, i.e. train our minds, then stress, anxiety and depression can get a hold of us. And even if we don't feel too bad for most of the time, we still find ourselves stuck in emotional patterns and habits, making us angry or short-tempered, or perhaps fearful. We seem to do the same things over and over again, like a fly coming up repeatedly against the same closed window pane, when there is a wide open door right next to it. We will allow our minds to run wild, pulling and pushing us in all directions, but will a little training and practice we can make our minds both strong and peaceful.

What Makes the Mind Restless?

How much of our suffering is caused by not having food or a roof over our head? For many people in the world this is a reality, but most of us are quite comfortable when we think about it. So why are our minds suffering? Why are they restless?

Often, it is our sense of self that creates seeds of restlessness in the mind. We constantly try to fathom out who we are, to define ourselves with certain labels. We end up analysing every thought and action: what kind of person would do that? Why do I always react that way? There is an underlying sense that we could be a better, more successful or more lovable person in some way.

We might be searching for our place in life, or

looking to put all the conditions of happiness into place so that we might one day feel content and settled, rather than all this constant striving and pushing.

Our relationships with others are a source of great joy in life, yet also a source of restlessness on occasion. There is the fear of being alone, and then the anxiety of losing one's own self in another. And there are the people who just seem to make us feel frustrated or rattle our cages and push our buttons.

For many people it is the notion of time that makes them feel restless – that there just aren't enough hours in the day, that they are rushing, either on an hourly or daily basis or that life was somehow better in the past or will be so in the future. There is pressure in today's world from all angles: from technology advances making us all available twenty-four hours a day, to juggling so many tasks in the day that you just feel exhausted all the time, to financial worries and feeling the need to succeed and live up to all the expectations of both yourself and others.

How can you release that pressure? How can you feel like you have space once again in your day and in life to breathe and simply enjoy, to get things done well and on time, to feel content, relaxed and happy? Once again, it really comes down to letting go, which we will explore further during the Mind Retreat. Because if we try to hold on to so many things, both real and imaginary, thoughts and emotions, fears, worries and expectations, then we begin to weigh our hearts down and make our minds restless. As we try to do far too much we then feel bad about ourselves when we don't manage to get everything done well (or at all) or we feel guilty that we aren't giving someone our full attention (instead distracted by a thousand other things).

Signs of the restless mind

Let's take a look at the signs of a restless mind:

- Being fearful or anxious
- Feeling rushed
- Feeling under pressure or powerless
- Feeling frustrated
- Being easily distracted
- Procrastinating over everyday tasks, both big and small
- Always moving on to pastures new
- Not sleeping well
- Not eating healthily
- Looking to stimulants as an outlet or way to relax
- Finding it hard to make decisions
- Lacking confidence; not feeling good about yourself
- Being trapped by feelings of grief or loneliness
- Always wanting more (more things, more love)
- Being highly critical of others
- Seeming to react very strongly to little annoyances

- Feeling stuck or directionless
- Being easily bored
- Being easily embarrassed
- Feeling under threat
- Feeling unloved
- Feeling that life is unfair
- Being jealous of others
- Always worrying or overthinking
- Thinking the worst

When we experience these signs of restlessness within our minds it is easy to get caught up in them. But if we can just take a step back from ourselves and give our minds a break, then we might see they are actually all things that we can change. We can't expect to 'fix' them in an instant though; it isn't a case of finding the right solution to each of our problems. We need instead to get to know the nature of our minds, how our emotional habits form, where happiness and suffering come from and how simple practices like meditation and mindfulness can be used to tame our restless minds and nourish the thoughts and emotions that help us to feel good about life and to cope with its ups and downs.

Restlessness comes from three main sources:

1. Physical illness and mental grief
2. Desires – being unable to obtain our desires, being stuck in a situation we do not like, or being separated from what we love

3. Our own sense of our 'self' or our personality
   – either an underlying sense that we could be
   a better or more likeable or more successful
   person or being very rigid in our own views
   and highly critical of others

Physical illness and mental grief

Physical illness often makes people feel upset in their mind or depressed. Even just being very tired can make our minds less happy or more prone to feeling upset or irritable.

When the body is unwell, often the mind struggles too, as the mind needs energy and vitality just like the body. Being inhibited in physical ways by illness can also make the mind feel hemmed in, especially if we haven't trained it to explore and expand, so that even if we can't go to the mountain, the mountain can be found within.

There are challenges in life that can be very painful and this book has no interest in trying to make light of suffering. But you may have noticed how different people seem to react to pain, such as a very serious illness, for example: some will live in complete fear of what might happen, of the suffering to come, while others will somehow find a way to really and truly start to live in the present. They will become even more appreciative of life, rather than focusing on the fear that surrounds illness or death. Sometimes this is a transformation that takes place in the face of a crisis, but often this emotional strength has developed through life – in much the same way that some people tend to see the glass half empty, while others celebrate in it being half full. We can indeed train our minds to cope better when the body is in pain, but this is more easily done when we are feeling fit and well, rather than at that moment when a crisis first hits.

The great thing is that there is always more than one way to look at a situation. As we have already seen, while you might be tempted to think that there is no choice in the matter, your reactions, your thoughts and your emotions are your own. This does not mean being completely unrealistic or living in denial. Acceptance is a key part of the restful mind. Often we grow up with the notion that to *accept* is linked in some way to giving up hope. But actually, acceptance is a great strength. When we are able to accept the things that we can't change, we no longer waste mental energy or anguish and instead focus on the things we do have some control over. By always remembering that it is with our thoughts that we create our world, we realise that we do have choices in life, even in the most difficult times.

Grief is always upsetting to the mind, but can also be a very beneficial process for people to go through in order that they may move on. But it is not always so easy to face such a deep emotion as grief; we might try instead to carry on as normal, hiding strong feelings inside for fear that they might overwhelm us if we let them come to the surface.

When we become stuck in grief or another type of mental anguish, it can feel like the mind is against us in some way. It becomes very difficult to pick ourselves up and dust our emotions down as the burden of grief, hurt or upset becomes heavier and heavier. Sometimes we hold on to such painful emotions beyond their time of usefulness. They are often the source of fears that get in the way of living as we'd like to dare. It's why meditation can be difficult for some people at the beginning, as they become aware of feelings previously so well hidden, or gripped so tightly – some good, but also some painful like grief or an old hurt. But then they realise they must've been there all the time – affecting their minds and life in some way. And even with this realisation the grip loosens, maybe just a little. Just by looking at the emotions within the calm setting of meditation or contemplation, they don't always seem so frightening.

Desires

Our beliefs about happiness can often become twisted and confused; you see it around you, rich people who still want more money, people who crave fame and then wish some days they could be left alone. In Buddhism we call these our 'hungry ghosts', and they will never be satiated (at least not for very long); not until we get to the root of what truly keeps us happy or in balance.

Somehow, we believe we need to arrange or control everything, whether that's material things or family, friends or work: if only we can get rid of all the unpleasant things and get all the things we want, then we could be happy for ever; if only other people would think of us in a certain way then we would be happy ... But thinking that happiness is attainable in this way inevitably leads to us setting ourselves up for disappointment and restlessness.

This isn't to say that desires can't be the source of much happiness when we are feeling relaxed and good about ourselves and about life. But let them get out of control and desires can make us grasping, constantly looking for the next thing that will make us happy.

Desire also creates a sense of attachment in the mind. Not only are we attached to our way of thinking and of seeing the world (we will explore the 'ego mind' later – see p. 44), but we become over-attached to the people or things we desire. We might believe that a certain person can make us happy, and conversely take away our happiness; or if we can just get that promotion, we'll be able to relax and enjoy life (but what about now?). If we allow attachments to become too strong, they can weigh us down in our minds and stop us from seeing all the other good things life has to offer, beyond our own desires.

I met a professor in Thailand who had conducted a survey asking, 'What do people want?' The most popular answer was, 'I want peace'. And he had smiled at this because if you remove the 'I' and the 'want', then you will have peace.

Our sense of self

Our sense of self has the capacity to cause some of the most significant unrest in our minds, yet also to develop our restful mind. In a way it is good not to be completely satisfied with ourselves all the time; if that were the case, we would never bother to look for ways in which to grow and become a better person. But it is when we attach our sense of self to specific emotions or aspects of our behaviour that we stop seeing helpful lessons and instead feel disappointed in or frustrated with ourselves. For example, we might limit ourselves with descriptions like 'I am shy' or 'I can't say no', then form attachments to these descriptions, putting ourselves into boxes rather than being free to be anything. If you recognise this tendency, then begin to think of your self-awareness as the beginnings of a positive thing that I hope you will see expand as you go through the book, and particularly during the Mind Retreat in Part Two.

There is a lot of pressure today to know exactly what your great purpose in life is – to have all the answers somehow to the meaning of life. And so if we don't feel certain, we may become restless in our minds, searching for something in all different directions; or perhaps we find ourselves making exactly the same choices at every turn, stuck like a broken record – we know things aren't right, but we're creatures of habit and it's never easy to take the road less travelled.

Sometimes, when you just don't know which way to turn, the best direction to try first is inwards – to learn how to listen to that quiet voice deep within you and not even press for an answer, just spend a bit of time with yourself. You might not always find an answer, but by giving yourself a break and your mind a chance to settle, you may see all of the good things that are already right on your doorstep. You might also turn to those people in your life who seem to be able to help you to see things more clearly and who help to bring you out of your restless mind and back into yourself.

Outer Ego, Inner Nature

The way in which we look at the world determines what we see. And every one of us has our own individual way of seeing, our own lens containing all of our memories and experiences and through which we filter what is happening in the here and now. It's so important to understand that our sense of reality is a *perception*; it is created by how we think, because this means that we can then also change certain aspects of how we look at things.

The tendency of the human mind is to see the world with a 'dualistic' view that describes everything through comparisons: good and bad, pain and happiness, beauty and ugliness, rich and poor. These are what our world so often boils down to. A constant inner dialogue is at work in our minds along the lines of liking or disliking people, things or situations, wanting people or things we don't have and constantly comparing our lives and ourselves to others – judging where we sit on the scale of who has more and who has less, who is more or less successful, attractive or happy.

When we judge everything through comparisons we feed our restlessness. We might work hard and feel that we are earning good money, until we meet someone who is earning much more than us, and then suddenly we feel poor again by comparison. Our circumstances haven't changed, but our perceptions have.

It is our *concepts*, therefore, that define us. We think we have to be very firm and set in our ideas, so that we will know where we stand and who we are. But then we discover that something that we perceive is great, someone else might perceive is just ordinary; or there may be a belief about which we feel strongly, but which our partner in life sees very differently and disagrees with.

In Western culture especially, there is even a dualism between body and mind: the flesh has traditionally represented the savage part of humanity, being sinful and weak, while the mind is sophisticated and reasonable, separating us as human beings from the rest of the animal kingdom. We have created a sense of separateness between the mind and the body, when actually, just like all those concepts and beliefs we develop and rely on, things are much more fluid and changeable. Just as the body can be weak, so can the mind. And just as the mind can help to look after the body, so the body can look after the mind.

In Buddhism, we say that our beliefs and how we look at our world are aspects of our 'ego', which takes up the surface of our mind, while our 'inner nature' is something that exists beyond any comparisons or labels. It's easy to mistake our ego for our true identity as it's so strong and usually shouts much louder than our inner nature. It is our ego that creates restlessness, but for much of the time is actually quite lazy, as it prefers for us to have rigid, fixed views of ourselves and the world, rather than being flexible and able to look with an open mind. The ego mind likes to know all the answers without asking any questions of ourselves; we are the way we are and everyone, including ourselves, will just have to accept the fact.

So the ego mind can give the impression of making life easier. We know our place in the world and in our relationships. We think we know who we are, and we can act and react according to the labels we have either given ourselves or have had given to us – how we or someone else might describe our character: we are quiet; we are shy; we are successful; he is the black sheep of the family. But if we shine a light on the ego mind, we can soon see why we might be setting our minds up for restlessness.

First of all, there is so little space in the ego mind that we begin to feel cramped and penned in. We listen to ourselves giving the same views over and over again, like broken records. We might feel bored in our own minds as we follow the same patterns of thinking; we can't seem to look at things afresh. The ego mind forms such deep grooves in our emotions that we can't help ourselves reacting in the same old way to the same old problems. This might feel ok for much of the time, but when we're not feeling so good, this way of thinking can make us feel bad about ourselves, as all of our negative labels become exaggerated and are increasingly projected outwards to others too.

But the ego mind doesn't like change; it is happy to leave things as they are. So even when deep down we want to change very badly, every time we try to start afresh, we find our old habits creeping up on us all over again. We might even end up describing ourselves simply as someone who doesn't like change, and by doing so, immediately put up walls around our potential to be so many other things: to sometimes be conservative, but then at others quite daring or adventurous. These labels we all use stop us from being able to learn and grow in our mind and therefore in life too.

Investigate 'ego'

*ego, noun, 1a. self-esteem b. excessive self-esteem.
2. the one of the three divisions of the mind in
psychoanalytic theory that serves as the organised
conscious mediator between the person and reality.
3. the self, especially as contrasted with another
self or the world.*
Penguin English Dictionary

Nowadays, when people talk about 'ego' they usually mean a kind of arrogance that is loud, blustery and full of hot air. Someone who is said to have a big ego is thought to be full of themselves, to lack the ability to listen, to always rush to be at the top of the tree and to think their own ideas are the best. The rest of us like to think we don't have much of an ego and if anything, we'd like to be a bit more confident and assertive.

But if we look beyond this idea of self-esteem at the other definitions of ego, then we find strong parallels between Western and Eastern philosophy. As the dictionary definitions put it, the ego may also be considered 'the organised conscious mediator between the person and reality' and 'the self, especially as contrasted with another self'. The ego is indeed very organised, putting labels on everyone and finding boxes for everything. It is through the filter of our ego that we give meaning to everything we see, touch, hear, taste and feel. It is a mediator that builds up over time, with each of our experiences going into the mix, as the labels that our parents and other people give to us become our own ego's labels. In turn, they become patterns and habits: the way we do things, the way we are, the way we think.

Our mediator as sense of self

It then makes sense that we begin to strongly identify with this filter or mediator. Our ego becomes our sense of self, who we are. It will often be just as dominant in a very quiet person as in a loud, seemingly very confident person, especially when it comes to limiting oneself with labels or feeling the praise or criticism of others.

And that is the crux of the issue, the seed of the restless mind. Our ego tries to make life a little easier by always seeing things in the same way, by creating a strong sense of identity to which we can cling, by which we can feel grounded and know who we are. But the problem is that this superficial ego – or filter – is so dependent on external conditions for its sense of security. So by defining our self through comparison and contrast to others we have, once again, set ourselves up for inevitable restlessness and eventual disappointment. Even if we are at the top of the class, we will, one day, come across someone more successful in life than ourselves according to our own set of standards, whatever they may be; one day, and probably on many occasions, we will disappoint ourselves or feel disappointed by others.

The weight of expectations

It is understandable that people are brought up to want to do well in their lives, to fulfil their potential, provide for their family if they have one and do their very best in life. But for some of us, the expectations and pressure to succeed can really play on the mind and end up causing a tension and tightness. And then, without a natural sense of flow, that pressure to succeed really starts to have an impact on the things we do. We might worry constantly about getting things wrong, fearing failure at every turn and every decision. Challenging situations that we would normally take in our stride feel like life and death in our minds and bodies. For some of us, this restlessness becomes too much and we turn away from success, opting to lower everyone's expectations and take ourselves out of the spotlight (the family spotlight can be one of the brightest). Unfortunately, however, the restlessness often remains as we wonder what we might be able to do if we could just relax and give things a try.

Doubts

Once the seed of a doubt is planted in our minds it often grows wild before we even realise it, wreaking havoc on our confidence along the way. And doubts seem to multiply: once we have a doubt about one thing, we soon seem to them about everything. The ego mind feeds on doubts; we start believing a very negative story about ourselves or those close to us. So we might doubt our abilities or the love of our partner. And left unchecked, this kind of restlessness can threaten the health of our minds. This is why meditation is so good for nipping doubts in the bud. We can observe them, noticing how and perhaps why they arise. It's not that we will never have them, but we will see them for what they are – something that feels very real but, like all emotions, does not have to become fixed and deep-rooted.

Our sense of others

Our relationships with others can be a source of great happiness, but also of suffering too, depending on our own state of mind. Our minds can get very caught up with how particular people make us feel, whether they drive us wild with longing or jealousy, or they just seem to know how to make us angry. You might think that as Buddhists we are never driven mad, but this is actually quite a strong theme in the philosophy – dealing with negative thoughts and people. There are people in all of our lives who are very positive for us and who seem to bring out the best in us. But there are also those – often who are very attractive to us or who we admire greatly in some way (take a boss of the company for example) who tend to bring out all our negative thoughts. We crave their validation or praise, or in some cases we spend far too much of our time thinking of the ways in which we wish they would change to make our lives better or easier. We take everything they say or do personally. The person in question might even be someone who for much of the time we love dearly, but then little things they say or do set off our wild elephant. Rather than take a moment to wonder how we might spend more time on what we *can* change, that is ourselves, we waste mental energy thinking about how that person makes us feel or how we can makes the planets realign to fit with our current idea of how we'd like them to be.

People often think that meditation is a very solitary practice, a type of 'navel gazing' in which one thinks only of oneself, and that isn't about real-life interactions or relationships. You might even consider it a lonely type of thing to do. But spending a little time alone with one's thoughts is very different from being lonely. Being happy in one's own company is even a part of building up your resilience and ways of coping well with life; and as it turns out, meditation is very much about the people in your life and your community, even the world. With loneliness, on the other hand, the mind almost aches and tends towards sadness much of the time. This might be a less frenetic restlessness, but we certainly don't feel comfortable in our own skins or our minds. We feel at odds with the world, an outsider. We might feel lost, unlikeable or unlovable. In isolation, these feelings grow and leave less room for happiness, self-confidence and satisfac...

The reason for loneliness is because our ego says, ' want love, I want friendship', while forgetting that in order to receive we have to give, and so feeling deflated when we are not constantly surrounded by praise and proclamations of love. If we can open our selves with love and compassion to others, we will realise that we are always surrounded by beings who love us and that all beings respond to genuine love.

External conditions

It is very easy to fall into a state of mind which relies on those things outside of us to determine how we feel inside. It is why a very well-known idea in Buddhism is to let go of praise and blame as both of these, good or bad, mean that we rely on external causes and conditions for our sense of self and our sense of worth:

The solid rock is not shaken by wind and so the wise are not ruffled by praise or blame.
Buddha

You might find yourself thinking that particular people or things make you happy or unhappy, not your own mind. You might rely on praise from your bosses at work to feel good about what you are doing on a daily basis, and equally dread the day you might be blamed for things going wrong.

up feeling defined by the words
others. We may be unsure as to
matter all that much unless they
n or admired in return. Rather than
ourselves in the joy of doing some-
w we're really good at because we love
it and hard at it, we become distracted and
unfocused as we continually look outside of ourselves
for validation.

When we can sit quietly and calmly and simply observe our day with no need for praise or blame, then we are beginning to really be in touch with the reality of our minds and our inner nature. And when we let go of the need for such external signals it's amazing how much space opens up in their place – how broad and wide our minds become. Being whole without relying on others doesn't mean that we are cut off from them or that we need to become aloof or like an island; it's just that we can spend a lot more time thinking good of others, rather than worrying about what they might be thinking of us. We can then equally let go of any urges to play the blame game because we are confident in our intentions and realise everyone else is usually trying their best too.

We look at the same world differently

Say you are trekking up a mountain with a group of people. For you it is exciting and pleasurable; it makes your body feel good and you enjoy the views and the exhilaration in every step. But another person in your party may be suffering from blisters or sickness, and for them each step is very hard. They are determined to keep going, but have a very different experience of the same situation. What is the truth? Both of these experiences have to be equally respected and at the same time ignored, in that neither person is attached to either. For either of them the experience may change in a moment, and so holding on to one truth or another no longer makes sense.

This is just a simple example, but when our ego is strongly in charge of our minds we aren't so good at seeing things from all the different sides. As we've seen, the ego is happier with the status quo than with being flexible and open-minded. If we have strong ideas about things then we often equate that with having a strong sense of identity. People who are able to see the other side of an argument might even think they are a bit of a pushover and would like to be stronger in their own beliefs; they don't realise what a great mental skill they have. Because those who are willing to see things from another perspective are the world's great listeners; they have great depths of compassion and empathy.

Of course, there is nothing wrong with having our own beliefs, our own way of seeing the world – this is all part of what makes us individual. Our experiences and our memories are within us, and the key is to be aware of the lens or the filter, to realise that we can also change the angle, especially when we are feeling agitated or stuck in life, that we can change the record.

The ego and 'attachment'

A key idea in Buddhist living philosophy is concerned with attachment and how it is our *grasping* attachments to certain things, people or desires that so often create a great deal of suffering or restlessness in our minds.

It's not that it isn't a good idea to form loving and caring relationships with others, or to have ambitions and want to do well in life. But rather, it is the nature of our attachments that is the key. As soon as they become grasping or driven by the ego in a possessive way then they become a potential source of mental suffering. This may just be in a small way, but it can be the trigger of real anguish. When we hold on too tightly to our attachments we are trying to keep them just as they are, to make them permanent. But nothing in life is permanent. Our relationships with people grow over time, jobs change or are sometimes lost, even bricks and mortar fall down eventually. When we come into our lives we are empty-handed, and when we leave it is just the same. And yet we seem to want to accumulate so much in the middle. So while it's no bad idea to wish to provide for yourself and your loved ones, one of the strongest messages I can offer is not to become rigid in your attachments to anything. If you can let things come and go without being ruffled you will soon begin to ease a restless mind.

Here is just a simple example of attachment. Let's imagine I have a very nice watch and I break it in front of you. You might say, 'Oh, he is crazy!' or 'What a nice watch! He broke it!' That's all. But if I give that watch to you and after five minutes I then break it, you might feel quite irritated or annoyed with me. 'Why did you break my watch?' Why is that? Why are you feeling the pain now? I haven't changed, you haven't changed, the watch hasn't changed. It is just an object, the same as before, but now that you have formed an attachment to it and consider it to be yours, suddenly there is suffering at its loss.

In today's world it is easy to become attached to wanting luxury. You might've been brought up to really make this one of your main aims in life. And it is very good to strive and work hard. It's just a case of being able to see all of these things for what they are. Having a roof over your head with enough food to eat is a fundamental need of all humans if they are to achieve happiness. But being very attached to anything beyond that simple roof and food can set us up for restlessness as we constantly compete to have better houses, cars and holidays. At some point, we're inevitably going to be disappointed and so we shouldn't equate these external things with happiness.

I am not saying that we shouldn't enjoy luxury hotels or that we should all be sitting in the Himalayas. But I think we should have the freedom to say: if I want to, I can stay in a good hotel and put on nice clothes, but I may also sleep in a tent with a sleeping bag because life is not constant and is not always steady. In fact, staying in a hotel is a good case in point. When we stay in a five-star hotel we enjoy all the luxury on offer while we are there, making the most of every minute, but when we check out the next day, we don't cry – we knew that staying in the hotel wouldn't last for ever. But with our own houses we often become very attached to them and suffer a great deal when we have to let go and move on.

As a spiritual guide, I go around the world listening to people's difficulties and try to find spiritual solutions for them. While there are many disasters happening in the world and much poverty, conflict and difficulty, a great deal of the suffering that I see in people comes from the mind because of attachments to wealth, fame or relationships. The grasping mind holds on to everything – beliefs, people, possessions – so that it seems as though there is hardly any room to breathe. And the grasping mind wants what it can't have, of course, always looking over the fence at what others have, always looking for more. We become attached to our own wishes, unhappy if we can't fulfil them, blaming others if not ourselves. In our disappointment we become irritated more easily, discouraged and even depressed. What started out as a simple desire becomes something that pushes us down through the strength of our attachment to it; we have made it a condition of our happiness, rather than something that might come, but equally might not. With so many attachments, life becomes heavy.

In the Mind Retreat we therefore give thanks for all the good things and people in our lives through the Appreciation meditation (see p. 102), while meditating on the nature of change in the same exercise. It is very good to love and care for people in our lives and to appreciate how our work has led to being able to provide for ourselves and our loved ones, while at the same time understanding that everything in life is subject to change. Nothing is fixed and so it makes no sense to become too attached – if we do, then when a person or situation does inevitably change we grasp at how we want things to be, or how they used to be. We aren't flexible or resilient enough to embrace change and so enjoy the moment, whatever comes our way.

We also look at our attachments to our emotions and whether we always need to hold on to them so tightly. By seeing our beliefs and labels for what they are – perceptions, rather than any kind of fixed reality – we begin to understand that we can be more flexible and open-minded; looser, rather than grasping. We don't have to lower our standards or throw all of our beliefs away, but we are no longer so arrogant as to assume ourselves to always be right, always the best,

ct. We can let go of such impossible ideals
t ourselves as imperfect, trying our best
an being the best, willing to learn from others
knowledge that sometimes we will make
mistakes. And by doing this we give ourselves a
wonderful opportunity to improve and grow, instead
of remaining stuck in our ways of thinking and living.
We can become fearless as we let go of our grasp on
the fear of failure, because failure too is a perception
rather than a reality. And when we loosen our grip on
expectations the world suddenly opens up and we
discover new paths that we had no idea were even
there.

Life is full of ups and downs. If you cannot accept
these things then when life goes down, you are not
prepared for it. All our lives, we go through so many
obstacles and difficulties. It is not the specific difficulties
that we should be focused on, but how we face them.
Because once we train our minds to be calm and strong,
we really can face anything.

We should have the freedom to have desires and
ambitions, things and people that we want, but we
need to be flexible and understand that everything is
subject to change and there is no point in getting
fanatically attached. With a relaxed attitude to these
things we can be as happy with a warm cup of tea on
a freezing cold day as with or without the latest
iPhone!

The habit mind

As we grow up we develop personality patterns and behaviour habits. Our ego likes habits because they are automatic, like all those tiny unconscious decisions we make during the day on autopilot that make life easier (how we are going to get to work, when to make a cup of tea, whether to eat that extra biscuit). But then emotions get caught up in this automatic process too, and emotional habits of the mind are created. We fall into familiar patterns when it comes to reacting to situations; we feel the emotions rise up and even wonder sometimes why we always react in the same way, putting it down to ways of thinking and feeling that are inherent to our personalities – something that we can't really change. Take criticism, for example, and how you tend to react to it. Is it a familiar reaction? Does your pride feel hurt? Do you always jump on the defensive or feel agitated because you want everything to always be just right and hate the thought of ever being wrong? And how do you react when things don't go according to plan? Do you always stick things out, even when you know deep down they are wrong for you because you're 'that kind of person' or do you run for the next thing at the first sign, so that you always seem to be running and never settling?

A scientist I know in Bhutan who studies happiness found that if you do nothing about a negative emotion when it first arises, it will begin to manifest more often. And if you continue to leave it untreated or unaddressed, then what started as a one-off emotion will cloud your mood and, eventually, become a part of your personality. So a person of whom it might be said, 'He is always in a bad mood', for example, didn't start out in life that way, but after a while emotions become ingrained and it is hard to shake off the labels.

Habits of the mind also provide our mental framework – the way we see the world. Making assumptions is something that humans do all the time to get by because we can't know every single detail about every decision or perception before we make up our minds. But our mental framework can become quite rigid over time. The most obvious example is making assumptions about people from the way they look, which is when mental habits become prejudice. But just as we might make judgements about strangers, we also make them about those close to us, and perhaps even more about ourselves. We put labels on to situations and people based on our past experiences, which makes some sense, but which also means that our view of the world can be quite narrow. This means that people and situations can upset or annoy us, because they rarely fit the way we want everything to be. We become tight and constricted in our minds, which can easily lead to agitation and restlessness.

The habit mind grasps on to familiarity, our comfort

zone, happy with the status quo even when it isn't very good for us. Often the habit mind goes unnoticed as we keep reacting to certain situations in the same way without questioning. It's just the way we are, it's in our DNA to act or think this way. But just as emotional habits are learned over time, they can also be broken, especially if you create a little space in your mind to make way for new ways of thinking.

It takes a lot of courage to begin to work with your mind and challenge some of its very set ways; it can feel as though your mind has almost been working against you for some time, fixing you in certain patterns of thinking, doing and being. But if you can bring awareness to your thoughts and emotions and really see which are helpful and which bring you down or make you restless, you will start to bring more balance into your mind, speech and actions and, therefore, your life.

Where do you look for happiness?

Happiness is a beautiful feeling. It is a beautiful mind, and a peaceful mind.

But this is how it often works: we want something because we think that it will make us happy. We go for it. We get it. But then it is not enough and it doesn't make us happy. So we want something else and we get that. We need something else again. Young people think that older people who are successful must be happy. Older people are still chasing after something to feel significant. So all our life we may be chasing after happiness and never getting it. And in the process, we sacrifice our friendships, our emotions and our health. People can end up sacrificing everything and not having anything.

Think how often you end up dissatisfied with the very thing that you dreamed about getting. Many people are brought up using dissatisfaction as a motivating, driving force. It's what pushes people to work hard, succeed and keep 'moving up' in some way. The ultimate goal in life is to have better and better living standards – a bigger house, a more expensive car. Our ego minds hoodwink us into thinking this is all we need to do to be happy. Either that or find the person of our dreams who will make us happy. The only problem is that because of our tendency to always compare, as soon as we get the thing we thought would make us content, the feeling never quite lasts and off we go again.

So where does your happiness really come from? Is it from these external things, or that person? Or is it something that is within you? And if you can start to see that it is something inside you, then can you also see how you might have some control over it, to nurture and make it grow.

Putting off happiness

Sometimes it is the constant chase for happiness that causes restlessness. Happiness is just around the corner, and we are so focused on the next thing, whatever it may be, that we forget about what we have in our lives right now, never giving ourselves, or our minds, a chance to settle. It's interesting because some of the things that can make the mind restless are not intrinsically bad; drive and ambition, for example, can help to keep the mind agile and energised, and it's important to take responsibility for one's future. It's when these factors begin to overwhelm the mind that they upset the natural balance and cause us problems. When we attach happiness to the future then we lose sight of the present for something that may or may not happen.

To be fearful or, conversely, very excited about the unknown is to be human in lots of ways. In most parts of the world, people are brought up to think often about the future, to create goals and ambitions according to expectations – either their own or those of others. It is important to be considerate of the future, but when we invest all of our present in our future hopes, we are placing a lot of value on what is inevitably in doubt. This sets us up to feel restless and agitated as we become dependent on an uncertainty.

I think sometimes that we feel restless because we have the sense that we are waiting for something to happen, but somehow we don't feel we are ready or we are nervous about making a change and what might happen as a result. We might not be very happy in our current situation, but at least we know what, or who, we are dealing with. And although deep down we want to try a different path, we can't quite make the first step in a new direction. What if it all goes wrong? There are so many responsibilities I have to consider first . . .

But having said that, few people I know ever regret taking leaps of faith, even when it doesn't go quite as they had imagined – because the beauty of life is so often in the unexpected.

Inner nature

Whatever joy you seek, it can be achieved by yourself; whatever misery you seek, it can be found by yourself.
Tibetan proverb

It is difficult to describe your inner nature as it is beyond words or labels, beyond comparing or judging. It is like a hidden treasure that is under the bed and which, for many people, goes unnoticed. But if you can begin to peel back the layers of the ego mind, to allow yourself to look at it from different angles, you will develop an understanding of what lies beneath – not only a mind that is restful, but one that is full of wisdom and compassion, and that seems to know the way. Your inner nature is your kind nature, when you give unconditionally, when you are inspired or feel truly motivated and full of vitality. Your inner nature is full of love. It is that calm beneath all the noise of your ego.

As Buddha said: 'The way is in the heart'. And so

if you want to have peace of mind, you need to listen to your heart or your inner nature. It might be a very quiet inner voice right now, especially if you feel that your mind is restless. But there will be moments when you know it is there, helping you out. It's when you are patient, when you can see things from more than one angle or point of view, when you feel like life is opening up and full of so much potential.

Now let us look at some of the signs of the restful mind:

- Feeling comfortable
- Being peaceful
- Smiles and laughter
- Tolerance
- Patience
- Focus
- Generosity
- Eating healthily
- Sleeping well and waking refreshed
- Contentment
- Flexibility
- Acceptance of life's ups and down, of the things we can't control
- Appreciation of what we have
- Being motivated
- Optimism
- Being spontaneous *and* well prepared
- Being open to new experiences

In The Mind Retreat in Part Two there are a number of meditations that I encourage you to practise to help uncover your inner nature and connect with it daily. And if all you do after reading this book are the Daily Breathing exercise and the Appreciation meditation for a few minutes each day, they will bring calm and openness to your mind and to how you go about your day. Connecting with the breath is a tool that you can take with you wherever you go to help in any situation. If you feel anxious, frustrated, tense or angry, then focusing on the breath will bring you back to your inner calm nature. It literally gives your emotions some breathing space and gives you time to consider your reactions – your thoughts, your words and your actions.

The Appreciation meditation is the first step towards allowing and encouraging your inner nature to come to the surface of your mind. Just a few minutes spent thinking about all the good in your life has an effect on your whole day. It is also one of the key mental and emotional skills used by those people who cope so well in adversity, showing so much courage in the face of illness or tremendous grief. They are able to find something or someone to appreciate even when life is incredibly hard. This often involves being able to look at situations from a different view, changing our perspective. It goes back to knowing that while we can't change many of the external conditions that life brings us, we do have control over how we react to them, and especially how we *think*.

Your inner nature is the restful mind.

2

The Mind Retreat
_____

*Our life is shaped by our mind; we become
what we think.*
Buddha

The restful mind is open, non-judgemental, curious, lively, patient and fearless. When the mind is restful there is a natural balance between the emotional and the rational. We can take care of everyday tasks, yet see the bigger picture at the same time. There is a feeling of harmony – that the mind is working with us, rather than running all over the place making us feel rushed and stressed and unsure about things. When our minds are in good health we will often tend to feel lucky and that we know our purpose for being here. We are nourished by our relationships and generous in return with our kindness and compassion for others.

This doesn't mean that life is a bed of roses; it is

still full of good days and sad days. But we have an inner resilience and appreciation of life, armed with which we can deal with challenges and change. We think less about how others see and judge us and have the courage to ask ourselves what kind of person we are and how we might improve. Likewise, we tend to judge others less and feel more tolerant and patient towards people – even those who manage to push all of our buttons. We still get upset, and we still get angry and frustrated when the world throws challenges in our path, but we begin to see those emotions for what they are: something that feels very real, but that isn't fixed and just as it comes it will go, so let it.

To have a restful mind is to relax in your nature. You get to take refuge from anger, jealousy, grasping attachment, pride and ignorance and find fertile ground for planting the seeds for ideas, making decisions and finding direction. But not only do you have to find the fertile ground, you need to plant the rice and do the weeding too. You have to nourish and feed the seeds of your good life, watering them with patience and kindness to yourself and to others. Let the sun shine in on your mind and your heart, give yourself time to rest and time to breathe. Make friends with your inner nature.

That is the focus of this part of the book, the Mind Retreat. We all have this restful mind, but sometimes our fears and our ego mind get the better of us and we can't see it. This is why it's so important to spend a bit of time understanding the nature of the mind and to develop harmony in it through exercises – in particular through meditations – that help to give our minds a well-deserved rest and to look at our lives, our selves and how we can make little improvements for the better, so that we can benefit everyone around us too. Rather than focusing on how to fix or solve the problems of the restless mind, we focus on nurturing the restful mind.

For many, simply giving the mind a bit of time off is all the tonic that's needed. The relentless whirring slows down and the mind begins to settle once again so that they might see things more clearly. Or they might use this time to broaden the mind and develop their sense of compassion and empathy – the ability to see things from others' point of view. For others, it is a very good time to 'let go', of old hurts and resentments, for example, or fixed ways of thinking – to be lighter and less fussy in their thoughts.

Giving the mind a break allows us to stop killing time with so much nonsense; we begin to learn the lessons of our afflictive thoughts and emotions and see them as wisdoms. We learn to become friends once again with quiet and silence, with nature. We rediscover our powers of concentration, doing only one thing at a time, but doing it really well. Through developing our appreciation we reignite our inspiration and motivation. We bring ourselves back into the sensory experience of the moment, rather than always thinking of the past or worrying about and anticipating the future. We begin to balance our body to balance our mind.

Tools of the Restful Mind

There are a number of tools we use to help us train the mind to bring peace, happiness and a positive sense of self and direction.

- Daily Breathing
- Appreciation meditation
- Contemplating Change meditation
- Self-reflection meditation
- Calm Abiding meditation: the mind as projector
- The wisdom of your emotions
- Letting go
- Coming back to the present
- Nourishing the body to nourish the mind

To help our minds, the very first thing we need to do is to engage with our body, and with the breath in particular. Just focusing on our breath for a couple of minutes is an instant relaxation tool for the restless mind. As soon as we bring a degree of calmness to our breathing, which is much easier to do than somehow flicking a 'restful mind switch', we begin to bring a little calm to our mind. By focusing on our breath, we also bring ourselves back into our body and back into the present. It is our body's amazing way of helping the mind out. We can then begin to use the breath as a visualisation, whereby we draw positive feelings inside as we breathe in and release negative thoughts or emotions as we breathe out. Just doing the Daily Breathing exercise for a few minutes each day will soon help to reduce your stress levels and increase your levels of calmness.

The Appreciation and Contemplating Change meditations are practised in combination, and are such a good way to start the day. The simple act of thinking about all the things and people in life for which you have gratitude is probably the strongest tool of all as it leads to so many other good things, like more love, more generosity, motivation, inspiration and kindness. Contemplating change is our tool for making sure that we don't become too attached to those things we appreciate! This isn't to say we don't care very deeply about them, but just to understand that we can't control them, and that anything can happen in life. What we appreciate can therefore change too – we don't try to fix anything, and we don't rely on certain things to stay exactly the same in order for us to be happy.

If you were to start practising just the Daily Breathing exercise and the Appreciation meditation combined with Contemplating Change today, then you would see an immediate effect on your day and very soon a positive effect on your mind. When you start the day from a place of gratitude, even if you have to struggle at first to find things to be grateful for (although you'd be surprised how they begin to flow), it puts you in a frame of mind that allows you to see the glass-half-full side of situations as the day goes by. And even if your calm is suddenly disrupted by a challenging situation, like a crisis at work or your toddler screaming the house down in the supermarket, you will start to find that you are able to let negative reactions or emotions come, but then also go a little more easily and readily.

We then delve a little deeper into the mind by contemplating who we are. We reflect on the kind of person we have become, our mental and emotional habits and patterns. This is not to find 'faults' or all the things we don't like about ourselves, but it is developing an ability to look inward and really know and accept ourselves, so that we can then truly get on with life in a very positive way.

As part of this contemplation we also learn to challenge the various labels we have constructed over the years – labels that have gradually constricted our view and therefore created a tension and tightness in our minds. We challenge our ways of always seeing things or people in the same way, including ourselves. This broadens the mind and creates a sense of spaciousness, promoting more patience, tolerance and flexibility, all of which are key aspects of a restful mind. Just as we begin to challenge the way we always think, we also explore how we feel, contemplating our emotions so that we might learn lessons from them.

It is through all of the mind tools above that we are then able to let go of the things that clutter up our minds and make us feel restless or unhappy or that we aren't a good enough or successful enough person. The restless mind holds on so tightly to so many thoughts and what-ifs that it can be overwhelming. Or we might be so continually distracted by all the clutter in our mind that we find it hard to get many things done in the day; there is no room left for focus, we're mentally tired out. Past hurts or regrets create clouds over our here-and-now. Or perhaps we just need to let go of having so many rigid beliefs and standards that we attach to ourselves and others. We need to live and let live a bit more. If we let go, who knows where we'll go – and that's the adventure.

It's amazing how often our minds drift in time away from the present into either the future or the past, so developing ways for bringing ourselves back into the moment are very helpful for cultivating the restful mind. This is everyday mindfulness; for example, when you are reading to your child you are right there, in the story and with your child, rather than thinking about your shopping list or all the things you have to do at work tomorrow. When you are eating you are doing just that, eating – tasting each mouthful, taking your time. It doesn't mean we never plan for the future or remember the past, but we remind ourselves every now and then during our day to be right here in the present, relishing every experience. We explore this everyday mindfulness further in Part Three of the book, applying the practices to daily life, from relationships to how we look after our bodies, to the restful mind at work.

When you hear the word 'retreat' I do not want you to think that by training our minds we are somehow cutting ourselves off from the world, or in any way repressing our emotions. It is more that we give our minds a chance to be reinvigorated, to look at things afresh and give ourselves the space to observe and explore. It is only when we take time to look after our minds that we have a chance to tame any sense of restlessness that we are feeling. If you want to feel more at ease in your own mind and emotions, then it is best to get to know what is there, rather than just feeling bad or guilty about anything you perceive as negative.

And then, as we become more familiar with our minds, we can see just where the healthy boundaries are, the places where we might cross from a natural feeling of joy into a more intense craving or desire. We can begin to notice where a positive set of ethical standards can become rigid fussiness, translating into irritation when anyone, including ourselves, doesn't quite live up to those standards. We can even learn how to use our bodies to develop our awareness; we might feel the changes in our breathing that signify panic or frustration, the heat beginning to spread through our bodies as we succumb to embarrassment or a flash of anger.

Why Meditate?

As the fletcher whittles and makes straight his arrows,
so the master directs his straying thoughts.
Buddha

It's funny how when our minds are restless we think they are doing so much and yet we may find that a whole day has flown by and we haven't found a few minutes to simply sit and let things settle. We hear about the benefits of meditation, but we keep finding other things to do instead. So we might have a glass of wine, switch on the television and collapse on the sofa in the short time before exhaustion takes us to bed – and this might help us to switch off for a while, but ultimately it is continuing the cycle of the restless mind.

It isn't easy to change old habits or create new ones, which is why it can be very helpful to go to a meditation group once a week to help you get started. And you could try making a pact with yourself to spend ten minutes meditating in the morning or evening. Set your alarm ten minutes earlier in the morning, so that instead of rushing out of the door you can take that time to engage your breath and just think of the good things in your life. You will feel the positive reverberations in your daily life from the moment you start.

One of the most famous parables told by the Buddha is the Parable of the Raft, in which he likened his teachings to a raft for crossing a fast-flowing river.

The story tells of a man who is trapped on one side of a river. On this side, there is great danger and uncertainty and on the far side is safety. However, there is no bridge spanning the river, nor is there a ferry to cross over. What is he to do? The man gathers together logs, leaves, and creepers and by his wit he fashions a raft from these materials. By lying on the raft and using his hands and feet as paddles he manages to cross the river from the dangerous side to the side of safety.

The Buddha then asked the listeners a question – 'What would you think if the man, having crossed over the river thought to himself, "That raft has served me well, I will carry it on my back over the land now?"' The monks replied that it would not be a very sensible idea to cling to the raft in such a way. The Buddha went on, 'What if he put the raft down gratefully, thinking that it has served him well, but is no longer of use and can thus be laid down upon the shore?' The monks replied that this would be the proper attitude. The Buddha concluded by saying, 'So it is with my teachings which are like a raft for crossing over the river, not for seizing hold of.'

Meditation is like a raft. It helps us to navigate the river of the mind and to get to know it, but we don't then need to grasp it once we have got better acquainted with it. We may float and explore our minds, and not drown in our thoughts, and then we need not carry all of our contemplation with us, but rather, we can leave it at the water's edge.

Buddha also talked about not struggling and not delaying with the journey across the river. If you really do want more peace in your mind, then don't put off helping your mind out. Go with the flow and you'll soon reach the other side. Allow your mind to fully show itself; you might be embarrassed by some of the thoughts and emotions you see, but after a while, you'll see that as you begin to leave your ego behind, there is no more need for embarrassment, judgement or intolerance – that you no longer need to hold on to all those painful or restless thoughts and can simply watch them and let them float away.

The word 'meditation' is not so alien now to most people as it once was. And many people talk of 'mindfulness' too, which helps very much to demystify what meditation is. Yes, meditation can be the practice of sitting in the cross-legged position as you focus on the breath, allowing the mind to calm, and I will explain a little more about this type of meditation and why it can be so helpful (see p. 91). But also, I want to talk about meditation in the broader sense. This relates more to everyday mindfulness, which is really where you bring the ideas behind meditation into your present, here and now. It is not about emptying your mind, which is truly the hardest meditation of all, even for those who have practised all of their lives. It is rather developing an awareness of your mind, and being more attentive in the moment. It is about allowing yourself to recognise what emotions are rising up in you and developing the ability to observe them, rather than be overwhelmed or engulfed by them: to know that anger comes, but also that it passes, and that you can decide whether to hold on to your anger for dear life, or instead to look at it, turn it over in your mind and let it fade away.

Meditation isn't something we do to become a 'better' person, but rather to help us better know the person who we are, inside and out. Through the practice we gradually become more comfortable staying with ourselves, instead of constantly running around in our minds, or trying to run *from* ourselves somehow. And then, we might begin to notice the little pauses that naturally occur; those moments when our mind is still, is resting between the usual constant conversation and chatter. This is when our nature reveals itself. And then, as we become more aware, we will realise when these moments happen during our every day – moments of complete relaxation or contentment, of complete focus or flow, of complete love or compassion. Our mind becomes crystal clear in that moment, as the usual clutter falls away.

But the practice of meditation isn't all clear skies and calm. Just as we can become more aware of positive things like compassion and love, we spend a little more time sitting with those emotions that we consider negative, like anger and jealousy. We learn how to stay with our emotions, instead of running away from them or sweeping them under the carpet.

If you are someone who avoids confrontation, for example, it is unlikely to be because nothing fazes or annoys you, but more probable that you fear the consequences of confrontation, and that you would rather smooth over the cracks and carry on as though all is fine. But if you don't allow yourself to spend time with your emotions, including such seemingly negative ones as irritation, disappointment or anger, they will gradually harden and sow the seeds of distress or restlessness. Through meditation, difficult thoughts and emotions may well rise up. And through practice, you can meet such emotions with kindness, listen to them, explore them and then really let them go.

Meditation allows us to see and contemplate the 'three things' that I talked about earlier (see p. 25). By investigating the seeds of our own happiness or distress, we may then, gradually, sow more seeds of happiness, tending and cultivating them. We do this through the Appreciation meditation and, as I have already said, if you take only one thing with you from this book, I urge you to take this. We can also meditate on accepting the things that we can't control, while nurturing our own responses, gently seeing our own way through. And we can also meditate on the nature of change and uncertainty in life. Slowly, we can loosen the mental ties between the unknown and fear. We can face our fears. We can let things go. And we can lighten our mental load.

The simple breathing meditation (see p. 89) is a

proven way to lower stress, so if that is your main aim, I would recommend doing this meditation once a day each morning and you will be helping your mind and your stress levels a great deal. If you want to go a little deeper and address your emotional patterns, then the contemplation meditations (see pp. 96–121) will be very helpful in giving you a mirror in which to see your mind clearly and calmly; that way, you can gently begin to make changes in both the way you look at life and your way of living it.

There are three key principles of meditation:

- Mindfulness – learning to be aware of our thoughts and feelings
- Continual watchful awareness – noticing thoughts and feelings as they arise
- Spaciousness – allowing space around thoughts and feelings and gradually loosening identification with those thoughts and feelings as 'mine'

Mindfulness

Some people find at first that meditation feels like the opposite of restfulness. They report experiencing a flood of thoughts and emotions, a feeling of being overwhelmed, a fear that they will never be able to calm their minds and that it would have been better to just leave things as they were, rather than let everything come to the surface. They feel they would almost rather be unaware. But by sweeping emotions and thoughts under the carpet we are not preventing them from affecting us.

It's said that the first step in making any lasting change is developing true awareness of what you want and why you want to change. And the same is true for the mind: the more you get to know it, the more you will be able to take care of it and transform things for the better. By becoming more mindful, i.e. aware of our thoughts and feelings, we are merely shining a light on them. We aren't forcing them into existence.

Continual watchful awareness

Mindfulness meditation is based on observation. We don't look to fix or find solutions to problems, we just look with awareness. If you have always tended to over-analyse every last conversation or situation, then this is going to be tricky for you, but incredibly beneficial. The key is to allow your thoughts and emotions to come (and go), but not to attach meaning to them – just to let them be. Your tendency is always to create a picture of the world based on analysis of your thoughts and memories, even in terms of how you might be able to make things better, but for now switch off the analyst and interpreter and just take note.

Spaciousness

I think for many people the restless mind can feel especially tight and cramped. You might have become narrow-minded in your view of the world or of people, or even of yourself. You feel there is so much on your mental to-do list that there just isn't any room left for creativity or spontaneity. The over-thinkers might cling on to endless thoughts in the belief they will somehow be useful, while others will constantly look to define and label themselves by their thoughts and feelings. If we can detach our 'selves' from the whir of our minds then gradually, a sense of spaciousness can open up, giving our minds a chance to remember what life is all about.

When are you truly present?

We are born living constantly in the present, rather than just for moments of heightened joy or pain. Yet somehow this changes as life unfolds, responsibilities get bigger and worries multiply, so that in most cases our minds are only brought to the here and now because we are either immensely enjoying the present moment, feeling relaxed and rested or because it has provoked strong negative emotions such as anger, sadness or dissatisfaction.

Meditation and mindfulness help to remind us that all we have is the present moment. They are literally mind training, giving our minds a break from wandering between the past and the future and allowing a sense of space to open up. And this is the space in which you find your courage and ask 'Why not?' rather than 'What if?'

> *When you sit, let it be.*
> *When you walk, let it be.*
> *Grasp at nothing.*
> *Resist nothing.*
> *If you haven't wept deeply, you haven't begun*
> *to meditate.*
> Ajahn Chah

There is a common perception that meditation or mindfulness are somehow designed to turn every negative thought or emotion into a positive, which is understandably quite off-putting. We do believe that our thoughts and reactions, and therefore our happiness, are always to some degree within our own control, but to understand the nature of happiness we need to understand suffering too. I don't think anyone can have true compassion for others if they don't understand suffering and so want to end it in whatever way they can. Life is about the downs as well as the ups, and to truly appreciate it we have to look the whole picture squarely in the face. And then, as we develop mindfulness, continual watchful awareness and spaciousness, we need no longer be attached to either the highs or the lows, but can realise that both are here in our life, and that both will come and go.

Types of meditation

There are three main types of meditation that help to bring us back into the core of the mind and body in a balanced way, to free the mind from constant distraction and to contemplate who we are and where we are going:

- Concentration
- Contemplation
- Calm abiding

If you purely want to try meditation to cope better with stress then the first type of meditation is very good for this. In the Daily Breathing exercise we *concentrate* all our awareness and attention on the breath, which gives our minds a nice rest. For so many people, the mind never gets a holiday. We never have a rest from living in hope and fear – the hopes of expectations and the fear of disappointments.

With the *contemplation* meditations or mind exercises we use the sense of focus created by the concentration meditation as a camera with which we can look into our minds. We go a little deeper and look at our life, thoughts and behaviours with a view to getting to know ourselves, reminding ourselves of what we have in our present moment to appreciate. We also become more friendly with the knowledge that nothing in life is fixed, and that anything can change, including our own emotions and the way we see the world. In this way, we become more adaptable – more resilient. We don't pretend there is no suffering in life, but we look at the ways in which our own minds are the source of our suffering and also our happiness. The aim of these meditations is to break down the wall of conceptions that we have built up over the years and, in doing so, to become less attached to our emotions and more *flexible* in how we see the world. We contemplate our thoughts, speech and actions, understanding that each of these is a cause that will affect our lives and those around us.

Calm abiding meditations take us out of our minds with one-pointed focus, usually on an object or perhaps a sound, like the wind. We go beyond labels to sit with the essence of something. Just for a few minutes, we switch off the constant whirring of the projector that is the mind constantly attaching meaning to everything we see, hear or feel. We allow emotions to *come and go*, neither accepting or rejecting anything – just leaving things be for a little while.

When to meditate?

I would suggest practising meditation in the morning because as life is a chain of events, we can influence our day very nicely by looking at how we feel and at our outlook in the morning. Aim for ten minutes each day, and after three to four months you can increase to twenty minutes or even half an hour. Even then, we generally recommend meditating for short periods with breaks, rather than continuously.

Some people like to sit quietly and meditate or contemplate, while others prefer to engage the body in a mindful exercise like yoga or walking. If you ask some people to simply relax in their mind, they will get bored and agitated, whereas they might love to sing or explore their inner minds in drawings or through images. Find what works for you, although I would also say to give sitting quietly a chance. In this hectic world there is hardly any room for stillness. If we can give ourselves these few quiet moments each day, then the world may benefit too.

Where to meditate?

If you can practise meditation in a high, bright place where your view is not blocked, this is ideal. However, if you can't get to a high place, the main thing is to feel a sense of light and spaciousness as this will encourage your mind to open up and feel spacious too. It will help very much if you can see the sky. We have a meditation in Buddhism where the aim is to merge with space, the reason being that we will then see just how small our own problems are. So being in a high place or one that feels light and spacious also creates a sense of perspective.

Concentration Meditation:
Daily Breathing

*As a single footstep will not make a path on the earth,
so a single thought will not make a pathway in the
mind. To make a deep physical path, we walk again
and again. To make a deep mental path, we must
think over and over the kind of thoughts we wish to
dominate our lives.*

Henry David Thoreau

The Daily Breathing exercise includes specific instructions for posture as this exercise is all about engaging the body to calm the mind. It is similar to yoga and is beneficial for your general health. It also allows you to really breathe deeply and take in lots of air. As the mind lives in the body it makes sense that the body can affect the mind and vice versa. So if stress and upset can cause physical reactions in the body, then so too can calm and contented thoughts (see p. 169, 'Feed your mind' and p. 172, 'Exercise your mind'). Really relax into your meditation, and don't worry too much about getting it right. Breathe gently, breathe softly and be very kind with yourself and your thoughts as you sit with them.

When we begin the breathing meditation it is like trying to switch off the television screen that is constantly running in our minds. For many of us, it is the first time ever that our minds get to take a break. Our bodies may get to have a holiday, but our minds are still in constant motion, even worrying about the holiday itself: what will the weather be like? Will the hotel be nice? What if we have to complain? Will we have fun? What will be there at work when I get back?

The breathing meditation is our chance to give our minds a real rest. It sounds simple, but it can have a great impact on our life and how we deal with everyday situations.

As we begin this breathing meditation, we bring our minds home, which is the present moment, here and now. It is also very important to understand the intimate interrelation between the physical body and the immaterial mind. The mind, at this moment, is contained within the body and therefore it is natural that the body has a strong influence over it. But we must also remember that the mind can sometimes have a stronger influence over the body as well.

For example, when the emotion anger arises, it physically affects us by triggering an increase in blood flow (literally a rush of blood) and rise in body temperature; we can feel the redness of our face. In the same way when we are calm, our heart rate is slow and breathing regular, our body reflects our state of mind. Thus the relationship between body and mind is highly inter-dependent on each other and being born as a human in this life, we have the precious opportunity to be able to understand and practise moulding and developing our mind and tapping into its inner potential.

In the Daily Breathing meditation, we use the breath so that our bodies may help our minds and vice versa, setting up a cycle of calm and focused relaxation. And so as to help with this meditation there are some factors worth considering when choosing where and when to put this into practice.

First, try to pick an open space and preferably on slightly higher ground, a gentle slope for example. This gives a sense of spaciousness that helps to open the mind. The other important factor is body posture. In yoga it is taught that when the body posture is correct, the nerve system aligns itself, allowing the breath to flow easily in the body which results in the mind becoming calmer and clearer.

There are seven basic elements to posture:

1. Cross-legged, with the left leg inside
2. Straight back, like a stack of coins
3. Shoulders stretched straight, like the wings of an eagle
4. Neck slightly bent
5. Eyes open, focused and downcast to about one metre in front
6. Mouth slightly open with the tip of the tongue touching the upper palate
7. Hands on lap, right palm over the left, with thumbs gently touching

For this meditation on the breath, keeping your posture straight, follow the sequence below:

1. Gently close the right nostril with a finger and take in a long, deep breath through the left nostril.
2. Hold the breath at the end of the inhale for a few seconds.
3. Close the left nostril, open the right one and breathe out of it.
4. Now breathe in through the right nostril, keeping the left closed. Hold at the end of the inhale and then exhale through the left nostril.
5. Next, gently breathe in through both nostrils at the same time. Breathe out with some force now to get as much air out as possible

Breathing meditation with concentration meditation

Here, while breathing in, we visualise that all positivity of the world enters into us in the form of a white wind. When breathing out, we visualise that all the negativities inside us – like anger, jealousy or sadness – come out in the form of a black smoke.

1. Begin with long exhalation through both nostrils – visualise all the anger, hatred, negative karma, disappointment and stress coming out in the form of black smoke.
2. Close the left nostril with your finger, inhale deeply through the right nostril and keep it in

the stomach for two seconds – visualise all the positivity going into your body in the form of white light.

3. Then, close the right nostril; exhale all the negativities through the left nostril in the form of black smoke.

4. Inhale one more time all the positive thoughts through the left nostril in the form of white light.

5. Close your left nostril and exhale all the negative thoughts through your right nostril in the form of black smoke.

6. Inhale deeply all the good and positive thoughts with both nostrils in the form of white light.

7. Exhale with slight force all the bad and negative thoughts through both nostrils in the form of black smoke

This is one complete set. When you are a beginner it is good to complete three sets of the exercise, then build up to more with practice.

The meditation on the breath is not only calming, but energising too. With practice, it becomes easier and the advantage of this simple but powerful meditation is that you can do it anywhere. It helps to sit in the advised posture, but it isn't essential in order to gain a benefit. So you can do this in the office, in a stressful situation or when you are feeling angry, sad or insecure. We think of this practice as bringing our minds home.

Sometimes we are here in the present in body, but our minds are wandering all over the world. This practice will bring the mind back.

This exercise can also be very helpful for people who have sleep problems. I meet many people who toss and turn all night, their minds in a constant whir – it's as if they've pedalled so hard all day that even after they stop at some point in the evening, the mind is still going, as if they are freewheeling on a bicycle.

When doing the breathing meditation you are not thinking about any negative thoughts, you're not holding on to any anger or disappointment in that moment. Nor are you thinking about beautiful things. You are simply bringing your mind to the present with no desire or expectation. The true power to hurt ourselves comes from the mind and our memories. An incident experienced long ago continues to exist afterwards in the mind, and it is our inability to let go that keeps us hurting. So as we concentrate on our breath, our thoughts get a chance to drift off and leave us in peace. At first it might only be for a few minutes, but as we practise the exercise every day, the calm feelings will develop and reach further for longer.

Do you have the patience to wait
till your mud settles and the water is clear?
Can you remain unmoving
till the right action arises by itself?
Lao Tzu, *Tao-te-Ching*

Think about how the water is clouded in a muddy pool. The only way we can see to the bottom is to wait for the water to settle, for the mud to sink to the bottom. Similarly, before we are able to understand our own minds or apply mindfulness to our day, we need to let our minds settle.

In answer to the observation that some people say they do not meditate because they are too busy, the Dalai Lama told the following story:

A monk keeps promising his student that he will take him on a picnic but is always too busy to do so. One day they see a procession carrying a corpse.

'Where is he going?' the monk asks his student.

'On a picnic.'

We often promise ourselves that we are going to do something – like getting fit, for example – but then seem constantly to put off actually going to the gym. The mind is the same – it cannot get fit just by itself – we need to practise and train. Don't put it off; go right ahead and start today.

Contemplation Meditations

Are you sleeping on the hidden treasure that is your inner nature without even realising it? Or perhaps you have a good feeling it is there, but life just keeps getting in the way of finding it? It feels indulgent to spend time with your mind when there are so many other things to be getting on with, and yet just think what a precious thing your mind is. Think about how much more effective we are when we feel at one with our mind, when it isn't racing, but is calm and focused, curious about what today will bring, rather than anxious.

By checking in with ourselves we can contemplate what kind of person we are and how we got here. We can keep complacency at bay by observing how our ego has been at play, and we can listen intently to detect that quieter voice of our inner nature. We are all used to having regular medical checks, but will often let our minds go unchecked indefinitely. No wonder they have a tendency to run wild and go off the tracks.

We are also very used to looking outside of ourselves and checking on others. Gossip is often harmless, but just think of how much time we spend talking about what we see in other people, rather than what we see within. And even if we *are* thinking of how we are doing, often we see this through the eyes and interpretations of others: we measure our success or failure at work by how much praise we get from our boss; we try to work out if we *are* a nice or attractive person by how popular we are; we hope that others see us as generous, funny and good, so that we might see these aspects in ourselves. In this way, we are checking ourselves against our ego, rather than our inner nature. We are constantly comparing ourselves to others in order to define our identities and to assess whether we are doing well or not.

An excellent way to peel back the layers of the onion and begin to really check in on ourselves is through contemplation meditation.

The breathing meditation is excellent for physical fitness or to calm stress and emotion. But with these contemplation, or 'analytical', meditations we begin to delve a little deeper into our minds and sense of self.

An absence of enemy does not mean peace – so when someone or something hurts or abuses us, then of course we are upset, we are hurt emotionally, but if we are disturbed and keep that hatred and grudge for our entire life, even when the person is gone, then we are the one who is negatively affected. If we can analyse and observe it carefully, and learn to forgive and remove the anger, this will calm us and we can find peace of mind. And this is how contemplation meditation works.

Most of the time we tend to use all of our senses and even our minds for looking outwards at the world. And so we begin to assume that happiness and suffering, contentment or disappointment, come from outside sources too.

We also tend to make assumptions about ourselves, often based on how others label us or because we have fallen into emotional habits and patterns that have become so embedded that they now affect our daily mood and even our personality. A professor in Bhutan explained to me how easily this can happen: say you are a very tidy person and your partner tends to leave their shoes lying around the house every evening. You put away the shoes each day, but begin to feel a bit angry about this, as they really should do it themselves. It's just a tiny thing, but if you don't do anything to calm your feelings, then each day you become a little angrier, and the anger develops into a pattern or a habit. You might even begin to feel the anger spill over into other parts of your day or your relationship; you might feel rather negative towards them over breakfast and start to notice other things that irritate you about their behaviour. In this way, your anger begins to colour your general mood through the day – you might be more easily agitated or upset. And, left unchecked, your mood can, eventually, change your entire personality. You feel you have become an angrier person, which is affecting your happiness and sense of wellbeing. And if you continue to look externally, the vicious circle continues, as you think you will only feel calm again if your partner would just change the way they are – which is something that you can't control.

The good news is that through these contemplative exercises you can notice when such patterns are developing and ask yourself what the real source of the suffering is. Can you look at things differently? Perhaps see that tidying the shoes, to stick with our example, makes you feel better, so where's the harm? And perhaps, as your partner sees how happy you are when things are tidy, they might even make a bit more of an effort.

Contemplation breaks down the barriers that build up in our minds between our outer ego and inner nature, and between ourselves and others. Just by investigating our thinking and asking ourselves where the negativity comes from, we often manage to remove ourselves from the negative thinking patterns and see things differently. We let go of our fixed attitudes more easily. We remember the bigger picture, rather than always getting consumed by the little annoyances. We become a little more relaxed.

We start with appreciation, then we contemplate the nature of impermanence or change, and it is then that we begin to consider what we have done so far in life – the kind of person we have become, the people in our lives, how we would like to be treated by them and how we would like to treat others. We contemplate our own compassion, without judgement or any guilt attached to the process. Because knowing if you have compassion is both the easiest and hardest way to examine yourself. Do you allow the pain and suffering of others to really touch your heart or do you sometimes shy away and instead look out for 'Number One'? And as you make room in your mind for more compassion, thanks to less worry and restlessness, you will also get to see much more easily and clearly where you might like to go in your life.

I went to the woods because I wished to live deliberately, to front only the essential facts of life, and see if I could not learn what it had to teach, and not, when I came to die, discover that I had not lived.

Henry David Thoreau

I think these words from Thoreau appeal to me because one of the most essential things in life that we search for is happiness, and we put a great deal of effort and time into what we perceive as essential to achieving it. But we often forget that the most crucial ingredient to happiness in our life is our self. Many of the things which we feel are so important and are the source of our happiness (or, conversely, that the lack of them is the cause of our suffering) are actually not the source. The source is our minds – or how the mind chooses to perceive, understand and project things. Therefore the development of our self (or, in other words, the development of inner wisdom and compassion) is essential for a happy life and restful mind.

Wisdom and compassion are like the two wings of a bird that is essential to every aspect of our life. On a general level, wisdom is understanding things from a larger, philosophical point of view, while compassion is the act of caring for others, putting our wisdom into our thoughts, words and actions. So as we practise the Appreciation meditation on p. 102, we develop appreciation and positive feelings towards ourselves, our loved ones and all the great things in our life, and so our compassion may grow. By then contemplating change, we are reminded that nothing in life is permanent, that at the beginning and the end of it all our hands are empty. There is nothing that is not subject to constant change, be it feelings, beauty, friendship, wealth, life or power. I think compassion uplifts us, but it is the wisdom that makes us understand the nature of things, so that we do not grasp or attach ourselves to things in an extreme way.

I want to stress that by developing our own happiness through the tools in this book and in life, we are then able to give happiness to others. As we begin to understand ourselves then we are more understanding of others; more patient and tolerant. If we open our hearts through these times of contemplation, then with daily practice it becomes easier to let go of the pain in our minds that we think has been caused by others. And as we let go, then our self, or ego, actually becomes smaller, leaving more room for others in our hearts. You might say that we realise we are all special and yet really not special at the same time. As you understand yourself, your ability to understand others with compassion can only grow too. And all of this is so beneficial for developing a restful mind. So before we begin these exercises it is helpful to make a couple of commitments to ourselves:

- May I develop happiness within me and give happiness to others
- May I say, do and think nice things

The mind, speech and body – i.e. our thoughts, words and actions – are considered to be like three doors, because through them we can be led to a wonderful place or a negative one. Therefore, we make a commitment to ourselves that whatever we do from the mind, speech and body, may it be to develop happiness within us and for others.

Appreciation meditation

Appreciation is a wonderful thing: it makes what is excellent in others belong to us as well.

Voltaire

I always suggest a very simple combination of two meditations to begin with. These are the Appreciation and the Contemplating Change meditations, which work so well together and only take a few minutes of your day.

I think we all know the importance of appreciation; there are so many proverbs that shine a light on it. With daily practice, the aim is to change our minds to make appreciation a part of our personality.

Gratitude is also extremely health-giving. It alleviates depression, makes us happier, improves the quality of

our relationships, is a good treatment for insomnia and
can help us live longer. These are just some of the
conclusions of a growing body of research . . .
David R. Hamilton, *Why Kindness is Good for You*

If you check your mind, usually you will find it's never quite in the present. It is still thinking of something that happened in the past, or is looking forward to the future – what might happen, what could happen. But life doesn't start tomorrow; it is happening right now.

So in this exercise we close our eyes and bring our thoughts into the present moment, reflecting on the positive things we have in our life right now. We start with our own body and then we slowly expand the circle to include our family and friends, our jobs, our community and the world. Often we have so much more than we think, but if we aren't aware of what we already have, then we tend to always be dissatisfied in some way, focusing instead on what we think is missing from our life.

Starting from good physical health, just the simple fact that we are able to see and hear should be appreciated, if we are able. Next, extend the appreciation for having family and friends. We are fortunate to have people who love us unconditionally, think about how they go out of their way to make us comfortable. Then expand the appreciation towards the world: good people exist to benefit others because the world exists.

All you need for this meditation is a quiet space, either at the beginning or end of the day. It doesn't really matter what you are wearing, but you may want to be in comfortable clothes, just to reflect your comfortable mind. Sit in a chair or somewhere you feel alert and at ease; it doesn't matter where in the world you might be, and there's no need to be attached to a favourite place or room.

Spend a couple of minutes focusing on your breath. Breathe gently and easily from your belly, your centre. Notice the breath, notice your belly rising and falling. Find a natural pace that suits your body. We contemplate and appreciate without clinging, without feeding attachment.

- Appreciate your body and whatever degree of health you have
- Appreciate the wonderful people in your life, who are kind to you, support you, help you
- Appreciate what you do, your career, your lifestyle, your community and beyond

Develop your sense of satisfaction. After all, what is happiness other than satisfaction, which comes from appreciation. Go into as much detail as you like. Appreciate simply and without any expectations or conditions; just appreciate anything that comes to mind for what it is.

To begin or end the day with appreciation may

sound very simplistic, but it just seems to work, having an uplifting or sometimes calming effect after a difficult day. It is not about having rose-tinted glasses on, but it is about finding the good in our lives, or looking at situations from different angles – turning challenges into opportunities, for example. It reminds us of the wonderful people in our lives and, in turn, how we might use our own skills or simply how we approach things to make a positive difference, today.

We practise appreciation for what we have because if you are not aware, every day, then dissatisfaction creeps up and that may ultimately lead to unhappiness. Every morning I try to appreciate all the beautiful people I have in my life and imagine how I would feel if they were to die tomorrow. This may sound morbid, but it makes me appreciate them so much more today. Sometimes I close my eyes and pretend that I am blind – just to feel how my life would be and how many beautiful things I would not see. If I didn't have my legs, my hearing, my sight, how different my life would be. I try to appreciate all the things I have. I'm not saying it takes away all of my suffering all of the time, but most of the time it is a great help to me.

Here is a story told from scripture by the Chinese monk Venerable Master Hsing Yun:

Rainy Day, Sunny Day

There was once an old lady who cried all the time. Her elder daughter was married to an umbrella merchant, while the younger daughter was the wife of a noodle vendor. On sunny days, she worried, 'Oh no! The weather is so nice and sunny. No one is going to buy any umbrellas. What will happen if the shop has to be closed?' These worries made her sad. She could not help but cry. When it rained, she would cry for the younger daughter. She thought, 'Oh no! My younger daughter is married to a noodle vendor. You cannot dry noodles without the sun. Now there will be no noodles to sell. What should we do?' Whether sunny or rainy, the woman grieved for one of her daughters and, as a result, the old lady lived in sorrow every day. Her neighbors could not console her and jokingly called her 'the crying lady'.

One day, she met a monk. He was very curious as to why she was always crying. She explained the problem to him. The monk smiled kindly and said, 'Madam! You need not worry. I will show you a way to happiness, and you will need to grieve no more.'

The crying lady was very excited. She immediately asked the monk to show her what to do. The master replied, 'It is very simple. You just need to change your perspective. On sunny days, do not think of your elder daughter not being able to sell umbrellas, but the younger daughter being able to dry her noodles. With such good strong sunlight, she must be able to make plenty of noodles and her business must be very good. When it rains, think about the umbrella store of the elder daughter. With the rain, everyone must be buying umbrellas. She will sell a lot of umbrellas and her store will prosper.'

The old lady saw the light. She followed the monk's instruction. After a while, she did not cry any more; instead, she was smiling every day. And from then on she was known as 'the smiling lady'.

Contemplating change meditation

It is not the strongest of the species that survive, nor the most intelligent, but the one most responsive to change.
Charles Darwin

The second step of analytical meditation is to understand the nature of change and the different types – small, major and continual. Most of us tend to see the major changes, like the end of a relationship, gaining or losing a job or ageing. But there are minute changes happening each and every second that lead up to these major changes. They are so small and so quick that we don't notice; every day our bodies change and yet one day we wake up and seem old. We look at a couple who have been married for fifty years and think how wonderful that they are still the same; but of course their relationship has changed in small ways throughout those years, through good times and challenging, natural ups and downs. Any relationship is based on the emotions of two people after all, and so can never be fixed in one place.

Think about how the world around us is changing every second. A good place to start is with the seasons – the changes in nature through spring, summer, autumn and winter; the change in the colour of the leaves, the temperature, what is growing in the ground. And just as every day there are changes in the season, the world changes, our relationships change, even our own body is constantly going through minute changes.

We use the following words to help our minds focus on the nature of change. You may want to say them aloud or simply read them to yourself, while thinking about their meaning:

- Anything that is born must die
- Anything that is accumulated will be spent one day
- Any gathering will disperse
- Any building will one day crumble
- Friends can change
- Enemies can change
- Happiness will change
- Suffering will change
- Concepts will change
- Emotions will change

- Whatever happened yesterday is today's dream
- Whatever we experience today is tomorrow's dream

To help with this we often contemplate a river flowing to the sea. We understand that it is always a river, and yet from each and every single moment to the next it is changing in some way – it is never exactly the same. Sunset or sunrise are equally helpful for this exercise as one is never the same as the next and they also remind us of the fleeting nature of time. And this is the truth of life – that there is nothing we can fix permanently: we cannot fix other people to be exactly as we want them, all of the time; we cannot fix our lives to be exactly as we want them, nor our minds. Things change, and that is why life is so precious.

One of my favourite writers put it beautifully:

We had a remarkable sunset one day last November. I was walking in a meadow, the source of a small brook, when the sun at least, just before setting, after a cold, gray day, reached a clear stratum in the horizon, and the softest, brightest evening sunshine fell on the dry grass and on the stems of the trees . . . It was such a light as we could not have imagined a moment before, and the air was so warm and serene that nothing was wanting to make a paradise of that meadow.'
Henry David Thoreau, *Walking*

This part of the meditation reminds us that what we see as constant in our lives or within ourselves is just a projection of our minds. Take a relationship we have been in for as long as we can remember: we might think of it as constant and solid, but of course, every day it is growing and changing, as the collective coming together of two individuals' emotions.

If we accept that change is constant, then we can become more accepting of it, more flexible and more adaptable. We develop our minds to be open to opportunities, more agile and receptive. We can also use this to understand that if we are going through a difficult time, it is not permanent and we can more easily let go of habitual reactions. So yes, that man made me very angry today, but do I need to continually grasp on to that anger or let myself go with the flow of the river, let myself change? Or perhaps I made a mistake in my work, I could get stuck in the guilt and embarrassment or gently pick myself up and be happy in the knowledge that of course I'll be doing my best today.

This meditation is very important in conjunction with the appreciation meditation because while we can uncover the unhappiness in ourselves through appreciation, it is an understanding of continual change that *prepares* us for life's ups and downs – no matter how hard we try to hold on, things always change. Likewise, if we *only* think about change without appreciation, we may begin to feel a bit depressed – if everything changes, what is the point of trying? We're only going to be let down. But if we combine these meditations, they create a good balance: we appreciate and enjoy what we have right now, while understanding that nothing in this life is permanent.

I find this meditation is very uplifting and teaches me every day how to develop my own sense of happiness from within. It clears away the clutter of the mind to get to what's really important. A great place to start the day.

> Restless Mind: what we have we forget to feel good about, then we regret losing it.
>
> Restful Mind: we draw happiness from what we have right now, and yet accept that all things can change.

Self-reflection meditation

I hope that as you read this book, you are beginning to understand your mind and your inner nature without being harsh on yourself or too critical. Just reading it alone shows that you want to improve your mind and your life, to be a good person to those around you and to appreciate what you have.

In this meditation, which we do with closed eyes, we reflect on what we have done so far in our lives. It is a process that helps us to understand the present situations we are in and to accept that it is our own actions that led us here. We reflect on the kind of person we have become: how did we behave and react when we were little or a teenager; what did we do last year, last month or just this morning? There is no such thing as a good or bad person here, as the true nature of being is always pure, but we can reflect on our actions and reactions.

To help reflect on our own selves, it is helpful to think of people in our lives, and to look beyond any labels like 'mother', 'husband' or 'boss'. Allow yourself to see them simply as human beings who also want happiness and don't want any suffering in their lives.

Then reflect on how you would like to be treated by others, and how do you treat the people in your life. Think about love, appreciation, respect, forgiveness, understanding, kindness and compassion. Just like the saying, 'It takes two hands to clap', we understand that people tend to treat us with love, kindness, understanding, tolerance and acceptance, if we have given them the same things.

This is a meditation that needs your complete honesty. It is not about finding regrets or wishing you were a different person. It is about accepting yourself for who you are, while developing the intention to benefit others in some way through all of your actions. This is a powerful and restful combination. Ask yourself directly, what is happening in your life. If you are ever feeling ill at ease in your day-to-day life, you need to understand the cause. We so easily miss these chances to stop and think – we are so upset we don't have any energy left to investigate. Try not to let your emotions drive you too far away from your inner nature.

It is human to sometimes get stuck in a negative situation and react poorly in the moment, but after reflection we may realise that we are actually a nice person who has just made a mistake. By accepting this, we can then take action to repair our mistake, rather than shy away from it, worried that we are bad or somehow wrong. We accept that we cannot change the past, but we can do our very best to make sure the situation or our reaction do not happen again and again in our life. This is the time to analyse ourselves and find our own way, rather than expecting or hoping that others will be the ones to change. We can use difficult situations to see something in ourselves and make a transformation for the better.

Equally, we can sometimes get on our high horse when it comes to how we think of others. We can become used to thinking that we are in the right and that our partner, our boss or anyone else is always in the wrong, making our life harder. Sometimes, we need to use this meditation as a form of mentally bending down. Just as we would like to be respected or listened to, we realise that others would like that too. And the more we can give those things to them – the more we can engage in our compassion and stand in their shoes – the more of these things will come to us. There is no right or wrong when it comes to opinions, so imposing our own ideas, rather than respecting and accepting other people's ultimately makes everyone unhappy. It is very important to practise listening, hearing and understanding other views.

Practice is about training your own mind, your own inner self; it is not about training others. It's is really about how much you are able to expand your inner space, so that the 'I' becomes smaller. If you constantly have this notion of 'me' and 'others', and you can't stop seeing others' negative qualities, then you have a lot to work on. You have not travelled enough of your own inner bumpy path.
Everyday Enlightenment by His Holiness the Gyalwang Drukpa

I love this quote because the end result of any practice should be to transform us into a better, happier, and more understanding person. In short, it develops wisdom and compassion. And such development is impossible if 'I' or ego is not reduced to a point where one at least has the ability to see beyond one's own desire and see things from others' point of view and respect the fact that all of us are equal in our desire for happiness and wish to avoid suffering.

Another reason why these words appeal to me is because they clearly point out that practices like meditation are for one's own inner transformation and not to become the authority on how wrong others are. If the end result of this type of practice is more ego-led and less about developing our compassion and creating spaciousness in our heart for others who have a different perception of things from ours, then what is the point of such a mind retreat? With such a fanatical attachment to one's own perception, how can our mind ever be restful?

Exploring the tendencies of your mind

In the Buddhist tradition, the characteristics of personality are illustrated as three pairs:

- Greed and Faith
- Anger and Wisdom
- Confusion and Balance

All these characteristics are in all of us, so it is not a case of labelling oneself as one thing or another. We all need to train our minds so that we may grow towards faith, wisdom and balance, and away from greed, anger and confusion. As you practise the contemplation meditations in this 'mind retreat', think about which characteristics speak to you – which you recognise as tendencies. You might recognise either the negative or positive side of the characteristic, and this can be useful as you become aware of how one aspect can be either a weakness or a strength for your mind.

A mind that tends towards greed has very strong attachments to both things and people. It may always be looking for more – more pleasure, more wealth, more love – and never quite happy with what it has. On the positive side, this means you can understand the concept of appreciation easily – that life is very precious and is to be enjoyed in the moment. You can be jealous and possessive, but that also means you have a great deal of love to share. The key meditation for you is to contemplate the meaning of change (see p. 107); to understand that there is no ultimate pleasure or measure of success that you can reach because nothing in life is permanent. And focus on your generosity, a great strength. Replace wanting with giving.

The mind that tends towards anger is more wary and suspicious of life, highly critical and judgemental. You might be a perfectionist who likes things to be just so and can be quick to irritation when the rest of the world does not fit into your ideals. This can place a strain on relationships, as no one is perfect and so will never live up to your idea of the perfect partner. You might hold on to old resentments or painful memories, clouding your enjoyment of the present, cluttering up your mind with overthinking. On the positive side, your strength is that you see into the heart of the matter, so can be very wise and insightful about situations and people. You think very carefully about decisions and know how to seek out positive influences to help make them. You are intuitive; you just seem to know what to do. The important thing is to focus on embracing kindness and love, grow your compassion through the Appreciation meditation (see p. 102) and let go of the past or always criticising others, instead focusing on your own actions.

The confused mind is easily distracted and influenced by anyone who happens to be there because they find it so hard to make decisions by themselves. You might doubt your own abilities or be quite self-conscious. You might think you'll never amount to much, or be conflicted about what you really want to do, so you put your trust in others a little too quickly or easily. But your strengths are that you have the ability to go with the flow in life and be easy-going, you don't have a problem with situations suddenly changing – you're flexible and adaptable. And as your ideas aren't fixed, you are able to easily see from other people's points of view, and so you have a great capacity for empathy and compassion and you can really get on with everyone as you're the least likely to be critical of others. The important thing is to show yourself the same degree of compassion and kindness, to see just how likeable you are. The breathing meditation (see p. 89) is very helpful because it allows the mind to settle and come back from all the distractions to focus on one thing at a time. Engaging in the mindfulness techniques are very helpful too (see pp. 175–257): eat simply to eat, or even as you do the washing up, just settle into the sensations of washing the dishes, getting back to simplicity.

Answering your own questions

The best place to find a helping hand is at the end of your own arm.
Swedish proverb

So many people are becoming aware nowadays that they would like to take steps to improve themselves and their lives. They are beginning to understand how amazing our minds are, and also how much care we need to take in looking after them – how stressed and vulnerable they can become. They are asking how they might become more compassionate, how they might find their purpose in life. The relentless pursuit for a better job, bigger house and list of achievements is wearing thin for many, as these things don't seem to be an instant fix for fulfilment.

It's tempting to go to gurus or experts for the 'answers', and yes, experts can definitely offer very useful guidance or information. They can help you learn and explore new areas. But it's important also to always look within for the answers to your questions. This is why, for example, if a person asks me how they can be less fearful about life, I can't give an instant solution. There isn't always a 'how to' answer. But there is a way to explore what it is that is making you fearful – to perhaps be more friendly with yourself and with your fears and look into your inner wisdom. That, I think, is where you will find the answers that are right for you.

It's the same when people ask, 'How can I be less angry?' or 'How I can feel less rushed?' The purpose of this book is not to wave a magic wand. True growth or change are not as easy or instantaneous as that. But by getting to know your inner nature better, developing your awareness of your wild ego mind, practising the art of the pause, I hope that you will come across your answers and really begin to listen to your heart. It's where all your compassion and wisdom lie, and it is with compassion and wisdom that life becomes so precious and the mind ceases to be restless.

You may have glimpses of this to begin with – you already have, I'm sure. And the aim of this mind retreat is to open those glimpses up wider and brighter. They are the moments when you feel content, inspired, generous, creative, relaxed, energetic and at ease with others and with yourself. Through practice, awareness, meditation and mindfulness, you can train these aspects of yourself to be stronger, so that you can better cope with the challenges that life places in your path. And you can indeed save your strengths for the bigger challenges of life by being more relaxed with the smaller annoyances.

> To be a little more accepting of yourself and others can go a very long way in easing a restless mind.

Calm Abiding Meditation: The Mind as Projector

In this meditation we look at how the mind is like a projector. Everything we see, feel and think is like a reflection in the mirror. While it looks very real and detailed in appearance, it is always given meaning through our minds, rather than being solid in existence. Say we are teaching in a temple, for example: to us, sitting there at that moment, it is clearly a temple, but one day the same building might be a museum or a hotel; it is various conditions that come together right now to say it is a temple.

It is the same for our emotions. We may go for a walk and feel very happy walking for a couple of hours, but then we are tired and don't want to walk any further. Now sitting is happiness. Then we sit for too long and begin to ache, so standing up equals happiness.

The essence of this meditation is, therefore, to think

about how nothing is fixed – not beauty, nor good, nor bad. And neither we nor our emotions are fixed. When we believe our perceptions to be reality, the ultimate truth, we constrict our minds and beliefs and then affect our actions as we continually try to make things the way we believe they should be, or suffer because things don't always fit our view of the world. Strong beliefs affect our patterns of behaviour and emotional habits, making us compare constantly and creating expectations and pressures to be a certain way, both for ourselves and for others. They are the strongest filters through which we see our world and attach *meaning* to everything.

The easiest way to illustrate this tendency is to think about designer labels. It makes very little sense to pay thousands of pounds extra for a bag made of the same materials as one on the high street, but if it is marketed well enough – if the stories we are told about that bag in terms of the talent of the designer or how we will look to everyone else when we are holding the bag are strong enough – then we will begin to believe it is better than all others. We will crave the bag and feel bad if we can't afford it or think that we aren't good looking enough for it.

I am from Bhutan and many people have labelled it as the most beautiful and happy country in the world. I went to university in Bhutan and now I have a retreat house there in the farming lowlands and I couldn't agree more, I am very happy there surrounded by the natural beauty. But it isn't the same for everyone. It depends on your perspective. Once I was travelling to the eastern part of the country to teach, and I found the countryside very beautiful indeed. I said to the local people, 'You must be very happy to live in such a beautiful place,' to which they replied, 'What is beautiful? Rinpoche? It is so cold here, nothing grows except potatoes, not even rice. Life is difficult here.' This was a great lesson for me. It makes me think of tropical islands too, where people will go for incredible holidays and honeymoons, while of course, many of the people who live there may be poor or hungry or feel their life is very hard.

All this is not to say that we should never want a designer bag or think of a place as beautiful, but the key is to develop an understanding that our happiness does not rely on these things – that we may be very happy on a tropical island or sometimes we may not be; it cannot be fixed. Likewise, we may have a very nice Gucci bag, but it isn't something that will bring us eternal contentment or satisfaction.

To take this a step further, consider the relationships you have and how they might fluctuate, even with the person you love the most. Sometimes they may call you so much that you feel a lack of freedom – you need personal space. Then, after three or four months, if they stop calling, you start to feel sad and lonely, so your concept of freedom or space changes. First you want things to be one way, then another. Or you might have labelled your parents as ungenerous or mean over the years, forgetting just how much love they did give you when you were completely helpless and needed them for every single thing in your life.

It's very human to want to describe people and things, and interpret their actions or meaning all the time. The key message is to be aware that none of these descriptions or meanings is set in stone – like everything in life and the world, they are subject to change. External conditions might cause that change, and we can also have the courage to sometimes challenge our own beliefs and perhaps be less attached to the labels we use, both for ourselves and for others.

My teacher His Holiness Gyalwang Drukpa tells a story about when he first travelled to Hong Kong as a young monk. Every time he got on a bus to go some-where in the city, everyone would suddenly stand up. He thought this was very nice and respectful, but that he didn't deserve for people to stand up and treat him in any kind of special way. Every day the same thing would happen and, eventually, His Holiness said to someone, 'It is so nice that people stand up when I get on the bus, but how can I say please not to treat me any differently?' The person replied that to see a monk was actually considered very bad luck, and that, in fact, people were standing up to get away! His Holiness always roars with laugher when he tells this story, as it is such a perfect illustration of how people see the same things differently.

If you are on a beautiful beach, you may want to try this meditation for a few minutes, or take a flower and focus on its beauty. Begin to contemplate that your concept of beauty is just that, a projection of your mind. Understand that it is relatively true, rather than a universal truth, and that any beauty for one person might be seen in a different light by another. Now, just look at the flower and do not label it as beautiful or not beautiful, but simply see it as a flower, accept its own nature. Leave it as it is.

This helps us to understand how we fabricate or label things – even emotions like happiness, pain, sadness and anger. When you are well practised in this meditation, you won't suddenly stop such emotions, but you will relax in the nature without rejecting or embracing, just seeing them for what they are – a wave that forms for a moment, then returns into the ocean, a part of the ocean; or a cloud that comes across the sky, but doesn't change the sky.

In this way, emotions, if understood in their inherent nature rather than grasped or rejected, are wisdom. Both positive and negative emotions are wisdom. They are a part of us, but we are not them; we do not need to be labelled or trapped by them.

Change the frequency of your mind

Many people don't feel they have the time to check in with themselves, to check who they are, what the nature of their mind is. We might describe ourselves as an emotion: 'I am an angry person' or 'I am a jealous person', believing that anger or jealousy is the nature of our minds. But think of how many changes our emotions can go through within just one day. So we cannot *be* anger or jealousy; it is something that comes, but it is *not* our nature. Such emotions are usually covering up our inner nature, a wave crashing in, but which is soon gone to be replaced by another. Most of us don't give ourselves time to look beneath our fabrications to where our uncarved self lies. This means we often deal with extremes – good or bad, happy or sad. We miss the middle path.

If you feel stuck about something, try changing the frequency of your mind. Let go of your old judgements and ways of thinking about the situation and open yourself up to a possible new way of seeing. Let go of any language that is keeping you stuck, like 'I always . . .' or 'I can't . . .' If there is something new you would like to try, be receptive to the possibility of it actually happening.

The Wisdom of Your Emotions

Your pain is the breaking of the shell that encloses your understanding.
Kahlil Gibran

Emotions are a part of living and being, but the key is not to be possessed by them – to understand that they come and go, as we say in Buddhism like clouds in the sky or ripples on the lake. We should be grateful for our emotions, as they enrich our experiences, help us connect with people and often bring us lessons, even when they are painful. But we should know that our true nature is not defined by our emotions, which doesn't mean we ignore or discount them in any way, but that we can feel confident and relaxed enough in ourselves to let them come, and then, rather than grasp on to them, let them drift away.

It is said that Buddha was sitting under a tree on the night he was to attain enlightenment, when bad forces shot arrows at him to distract him and prevent this from happening. His mind was so aware and so open, however, that he was able to turn the arrows into flowers.

The same can be said of our own minds and whether we allow our emotions to be arrows that might hurt us, or practise turning them into flowers. As we develop our awareness, we can begin to stop anger in its tracks or turn jealousy into caring and compassion, for example.

The five main 'afflictive' emotions are:

- anger
- pride
- jealousy
- attachment
- misunderstanding

Anger

Holding on to anger is like grasping on to a hot coal.
Buddha

Anger destroys our peaceful state of mind. When we are angry, we lose the power to reason, to the extent that if two people who are arguing become angry, they will soon forget what they started arguing about in the first place.

While it is impossible to subdue the things outside of us that have the potential to trigger our anger, it is easier and possible to subdue that anger within one's own mind.

You will not become ugly if someone tells you so, nor will you become a thief if someone accuses you of stealing. So why become so upset or defensive? If another person directs their anger towards you, you might try to practise compassion instead by understanding that their anger has taken them out of their own state of mind, so that they are unable to be reasonable. It may not be easy, but it is up to you whether or not you follow them into anger and away from your own nature or practise a different response. And when you see the results of controlling your anger – how much peace of mind you will get, how much better you will get along with your family, how calm you are in situations that once made you so irritated and how much love you receive – I hope you will want to keep practising.

With just a few minutes' meditation each day, you will discover that a new sense of relaxation will begin to grow in your mind. As you contemplate the coming and going of emotions, you will find that extra breath needed to pause in the heat of the moment and see your anger or frustration for what they are, rather than becoming so consumed by them. The aim is to suspend judgement and, instead, simply observe. Gradually, with practice, you may then find that in day-to-day life you can put judgement aside more often and be more accepting.

> The antidotes for anger are compassion and tolerance.

Pride

When you realise that there is someone who is richer than you, better looking than you, more popular than you, your pride is hurt and you become unhappy. Listen to yourself and check how often you say or think things like, 'If I were organising this task, it would be much better'; 'If we did things my way, we would make much more of a success of it'; 'If I were the manager of this shop/restaurant/business, I would do things differently.' It is very easy to fall for our own idea of being better or the best. Our ego takes over and squeezes out everyone else's ideas. But if we always think we are right or the best then we don't leave ourselves any room for growth or improvement and can become stuck, fixed in our own narrow beliefs, shutting ourselves off from learning and opportunity. If we are full of pride we can also become frustrated very easily, not believing others to be good enough, wanting the world to just fall into step with our own ways of thinking and doing.

Never be afraid to ask, 'Am I that good?' or 'What do I really know?' if your ego is running away with itself. You cannot become the best in everything, so it is easier to be humble. It might seem like people with lots of pride in themselves are perfectly happy being unaware, and that they glide through life enjoying everything, while those who are trying their best to be good to others are less happy, as they see all their negative emotions and always want to improve. Doubts about the self are honest, they are inevitable. If you are not ignoring them, then you are becoming more aware and have the potential not only for growth, but for a restful, happier mind in the long run.

Humility is the antidote to pride. In the long run it is the humble person who gains respect.

Jealousy

None of us has moved very far from the seven-year-old who vigilantly watches to see who got more.
Mark Epstein, *Thoughts Without a Thinker*

Jealousy is the thought that stops us from enjoying what we have. In the process of worrying and trying to achieve what others have, we cannot relish what we already possess. Feelings of jealousy make the mind disturbed and restless and are a good sign that we really need to turn the spotlight away from others and on to ourselves. What is the source of the insecurity that is making us envy someone else, rather than celebrate and support them?

It is important to do positive things with the motivation of benefiting others, rather than from a motivation of jealousy. Jealousy will turn a positive action into a negative one through the intention. Let go of the drive to always outdo others.

> To rejoice in the happiness and good qualities of others is the antidote to jealousy and doing so will allow our mind to relax and enjoy what we have.

Attachment

Attachment comes from a 'me-and-mine' state of mind – my house, my family, my friend, my lover and so on.

The false sense of permanence behind the feeling of attachment is very strong. Also, we are attached to the concept of how we want things to be. So when a person or thing departs from the ideal or personality with which we have associated it – be it friend, father, lover – then suffering comes. By understanding the impermanent nature of everything, however, we can minimise the strength of any expectations we may have of a situation or people (including ourselves) to be a certain way and develop a sense of contentment.

> Reflect on your body, emotions, relationships, opinions, status, weather, time – you will realise that all are impermanent. Understanding this is the antidote to attachment.

Misunderstanding

The main cause of mental suffering is misunderstanding – that is thinking that everything exists exactly as we perceive it. There is an old Buddhist story about a man walking home one evening. In the dim light of dusk he sees a snake on the path just ahead of him and starts, very fearful, his heart beating and his mind alert. But on closer reflection he realises he was mistaken – it is not a snake, but a rope. Relieved and laughing at himself, he steps over the rope and, as he does so, he looks down and sees it is, in fact, a necklace of jewels! It is natural that we make assumptions in our own lives, but without understanding we take all of our presumptions to be reality. And in so doing we might miss the string of jewels that is right in front of us, thinking it to be a snake!

Even 'good' and 'bad' are reflections of our own perception. So someone who is a good friend and good person to you can be a bad person and enemy to someone else. By grasping on to your own perception of what is reality, then the other afflictive emotions are more likely to come up. But understanding everything to be a reflection of your own mind and becoming less fanatical about everything is a key to the restful mind. Right now, most of us are fanatics in one way or another. We are very attached to our concepts of good and bad, beautiful or ugly, our likes and dislikes.

Wisdom and compassion are the antidote to misunderstanding.

In developing our minds we can begin to find the antidotes to these disturbing states of mind. But as long as our minds are controlled by these five 'poisons' we can never be truly happy or have peace of mind.

If we can minimise our negative thoughts and actions, we can begin to clear our minds and create a space for greater understanding of life without all the usual fabrications. The easiest way to do this is by developing our capacity for positive thoughts and actions, and one of the strongest positive thoughts of all is love and compassion for others. Because when you love someone, you think less of yourself and become a little selfless as you wish to give happiness to the other person. As long as that thought lasts, so does happiness.

As you extend this love for one person outwards to include family and friends, colleagues, neighbours and, gradually, all people, there is less and less room for the afflictive emotions. We appreciate our parents for the love and kindness of giving us life and bringing us up in this world. And then as we develop our respect for our parents, teachers, elders and gradually all others, we begin to create a society where we will also be respected and loved in return.

Don't ignore your emotions

Non-judgemental awareness of emotions gives us freedom from them. If we are always made to feel shame or guilt about our emotions, then we won't be able to look at them very clearly and will find it much harder to let go of them. Emotions that are repressed are still very much there, bubbling away beneath the surface, and if we try to ignore or push down those that we do not like in ourselves, then in a way we become bound to them and they become obstacles or blocks to our enjoyment of life. They create a restless-ness in our minds and in our hearts. Likewise, when we give ourselves over to such emotions as pride or anger, we become trapped in them, feeling that we are the emotion itself: 'I am angry'.

> The language of emotions:
>
> • Restless mind says: I am angry.
> • *Restful mind says: I feel anger.*

Make the most of your regrets; never smother your sorrow, but tend and cherish it till it comes to have a separate and integral interest. To regret deeply is to live afresh.
Henry David Thoreau

Some people say that when they do meditation, they feel a great many difficult or upsetting emotions, whereas if they do not do meditation, they feel better, less vulnerable. It's as though meditation feels like opening up a can of worms. But without this awareness there cannot be true restfulness or relaxation. You are just covering up. If you can become aware, then you can be truly relaxed and confident in your nature; you will know deep down that you really are a nice and good person.

Our emotions are a doorway to wisdom, connection and compassion. They allow us to feel pain, to care deeply, to put ourselves in others' shoes, to fall in love, be inspired and do great work. They can even be a support and path to understanding – they are a key to knowing who we are. Life is created by desire, which is why it is so important to have an understanding. Desire can be a beautiful thing, but just ask yourself where it is coming from. Is it to help others, to inspire, to have an appreciation of life? Or is it filled with attachment? Look directly at your emotions, look from all sides. Check in on yourself and find out where it has come from, what is it about? Did you see it coming and what can it teach you?

If we don't give ourselves time to relax and peel away the fabrications of our minds, then we might write ourselves off, saying, 'I am a very angry person' or 'I am a very jealous person'. If we can look inwards we can see that while those emotions do exist in our mind, they are not our nature, certainly not twenty-four hours a day, 365 days of the year. Things aren't so black and white.

The Art of Letting Go

In the end these things matter most: how well did you love? How fully did you live? How deeply did you let go?
Buddha

It's one thing to embrace the idea that we might need to let go of something – whether it's a past hurt that is continuing to impact on our emotions or life in a way that isn't helping us, a label with which we box ourselves in or even a person who we can tell deep down is a negative influence on us. It's quite another, however, to then go ahead and do it.

In beginning to understand that not all of our emotional habits are helpful, you have already taken the first step. You are beginning to listen to your inner wisdom, rather than let your ego mind continually run the show. It's not to say that the emotions themselves are in some way 'bad'; we've seen that all emotions are our teachers and add colour and depth to life. But it is the way in which we react to our feelings that may allow them to ruin our day or even very long periods of our lives. What kind of meaning do we attach to them? How long do we cling to them when the moment has clearly passed for everyone else?

As your awareness develops through your everyday experience and also the meditation and mindfulness practices, you will begin to notice a tiny gap between your emotions and your reactions. Be very patient with yourself as you begin this process of heightening your awareness. At first it is a case of really noticing when you have afflictive emotions, both those that seem to bubble up very quickly out of nowhere in reaction to a situation or person and those that quietly eat away at your confidence and self-esteem. For some, this might be anger, perhaps being very oversensitive to something, or a surge of jealousy as a friend tells you of their success or a lover glances across the room at another. For others it might be a more general feeling of somehow being unlovable, or that they have always been 'good', and so whatever they do there is an intense anxiety about the possibility of failing. We will look at all of these in detail over the next few pages.

You won't suddenly stop having negative emotions or reactions, but you can begin to observe them – at first after they have already appeared and then, gradually, as they come or as your body and mind give you tell-tale signs that they are about to surface. Ask yourself, with no sense of judgement, where did they come from? Perhaps there was another trigger involved, which you hadn't initially thought of – say, you were hungry or very tired. Ask yourself if your ego might be involved in the emotion – are you taking things rather personally and putting yourself at the centre of the universe?

Remember that when we debate and discuss ideas with other people we don't always accept what they say without question. We explore and we ask for more information, so that we might see things from their alternative point of view. And we can do the same with our own minds. Just asking a few simple questions like this often helps to take the intensity out of the feelings, and you have begun to let go without even realising it.

Or you might still feel the initial reaction was understandable in the circumstances, but by looking at it you accept that holding on to the feeling is making you rather uncomfortable and ruining your day. You remember the Appreciation and Contemplating Change meditations (see pp. 102 and 107 respectively) and think: well, that wasn't so great, but I don't have to stay stuck in the painful feeling; I have all these other good feelings I can access too.

Sometimes we are a little afraid of letting go; for example when we are faced with a dilemma or difficult life choice. We might hold off making a decision even until it is too late, as we were so distracted by worrying about the consequences. At other times it is emotions or labels that we have become very attached to (that is, projection of the mind). We believe strongly that certain characteristics or weaknesses are an inherent part of our personalities: they are who we are. For example, if you are quick to anger and so are described as fiery and passionate, you may worry that letting go of that anger will mean you lose a part of yourself – that you might not know who you are without it. But it is not the anger itself that you are letting go of, rather your reaction to it – the 'what-you-do-next' part. Emotions are very much a part of us, our humanity, but we don't need to cling to them to be ourselves.

Letting go of deep hurts or labels with which you have lived almost your entire life is not easy and can often require professional counselling or therapy. But going some way to understanding how your mind works yourself can also be of help here. It is then possible to gently let go of unhelpful patterns and emotional habits, while keeping all the valuable parts. Yes, your ego mind will certainly miss behaving in the same old familiar way and might kick and scream occasionally. But gradually, you will feel that wrench in the pit of your stomach or that constant whirring and analysing of the mind with less frequency and the weight on your shoulders will release. Your sense of life lightens and gives you the chance to focus and joyfully get on with things that make a difference, that matter and remind you what life is all about.

Letting go of anger

Anger is a good example to start with because it is such a strong emotion and something that so many people really don't want to hold on to.

Buddha said that anger was like picking up a hot coal with the intent to throw it at someone, but the person who really gets hurt is you. There are times, of course, when it is very natural to be angry and it would be unhealthy not to express or allow yourself to feel this strong emotion. But just as it is natural to experience anger in your mind, it is good to develop an awareness about whether anger is ever very helpful and to ask if it really makes you feel good or, instead, brings pain, upset and restlessness.

As you begin to develop your concentration of the mind and you are able to look inwards to contemplate the kind of person you are, then you will begin to have the time and distance you need to look at your anger, rather than always be consumed by it in the moment. If you don't give your mind any training, then an emotion like anger will easily control you as it is very good at catching you unawares. You might even be aware of your quick temper, but feel powerless to do anything about it, as there is no time to check where it has actually come from in the heat of reacting to a particular situation. So at first, don't try to suppress your anger when it comes, but begin to notice it and observe its source and characteristics. Why do certain things seem to press your buttons, while others do not? What is it that really gets to you? Is it rudeness, for example? Or if, say, someone is mean-spirited in some way, do you feel affronted by their words or actions? How could they do that? How could they say that? Or perhaps it is when you feel powerless in a situation: when the bus drives off just as you get to the stop; your boss overlooks you for the promotion you have been working so hard for; the bank sends you a letter to inform you that your mortgage interest is suddenly going to rise beyond your current means; you are exhausted and then your teenage child decides on this particular night to stay out at a party until the small hours as you wait up, worried at home. All of these things can be triggers for feelings of anger.

This is life in the real world and it doesn't exactly always go to plan. Some days, we even feel like the whole world is against us. But it's what we do with our anger that makes the difference between picking up the hot coal and burning ourselves and allowing it to cool down. So if a colleague or your partner has done something that has made your day much harder than it needed to be and you are feeling furious with them, you may scream and shout in anger. But what response does that usually elicit? Perhaps you end up making them angry too, or they feel embarrassed and very bad about what they have done, to the point that they get very upset or want to leave. Alternatively, you might remain quiet, but your anger is still right there, simmering so close to the surface that everyone around you can feel it. You are still holding the hot coal. So when you feel the burn, perhaps you might throw the coal down instead of throwing it at someone else, and take a little time to look at it – to try and articulate it. Question why you feel the anger, and where it has come from. Perhaps a combination of external factors and conditions within yourself are playing a part too – like tiredness or maintaining very exacting standards, wanting things to be just so.

Finding the balance between speaking up in an assertive, helpful way and using words as daggers against another isn't always easy, but it is worth practising for our own restful minds and for the happiness of those around us. At the beginning it might be very difficult for you to control your temper, but when you begin to see the results – the peace of mind you will get, how much better you will get along with your family, friends, colleagues or even strangers on the street – you will know it is worth the practice.

A number of the practices in this book are particularly helpful for letting go of anger. Simply focusing on the breath (see p. 89 for a few moments when you feel the burn of anger can cool the flames by lowering your heart rate, calming the body to help calm the mind.

The Appreciation meditation (see p. 102) helps to reframe the mind with a more positive outlook on life; by focusing on the ups, we have more resilience for the downs, and so will perhaps be less quick to grasp at anger.

Contemplating change (see p. 107) is also very helpful, as we develop our sense of going with the flow, going around obstacles and taking them more in our stride, rather than always bumping up against the boulders.

It's also good to think about how we might help ourselves to be a little less rushed during our day, so that we have more time and space in which to let anger cool off. A tip for getting up earlier in the morning is to do so gradually, a few minutes earlier each day, rather than trying to get up an hour earlier all in one go. Getting a good night's sleep (see p. 191) also helps us to feel refreshed and often less easily agitated.

Spending time looking inwards, contemplating the self (see p. 74), allows us to explore our anger in a way that looks at where it comes from *within* us, rather than just putting labels on the various external conditions that 'make' us angry. Are we someone who likes things to be just so and there-fore might benefit from encouraging ourselves to look at things from different perspectives (see p. 42), or perhaps we have more general frustrations about life that make us quick to anger. For example, we might be unhappy about work and exploring this helps us to realise why we are always complaining about our journey there; or we have a general anxiety about our finances, so we become unreasonably angry when our partner treats themselves to a new pair of shoes.

Letting go of fear

It is said that all of our fears boil down to three things: other people, death and our own minds. We fear what other people may do to us – how they might make us feel through their actions or words, their praise or blame, the fear we might be abandoned or left alone, the fear of being unlovable – and we fear what they may think of us, what they might say about us when we are not there.

Death is the fear that so many people today never address and yet it is the one certainty we have in life. Our ego mind seeks security and safety, so it makes sense that death is so often the biggest fear of all and something for which we do so little to prepare in our minds. In Buddhism a great deal of emphasis is placed on having a good life, so that we might have a good death, and to do this we must be accepting of death, using that certainty to motivate us through our present life.

And the fear of our own minds is at the heart of

this book. I hope that it may in some way help you to become friendly with your own mind, to see that it is your ally and not your enemy. Don't be afraid to look at your mind full on; don't be frightened of what you might discover. That is your ego talking. Even if you find suffering in your mind, it is better to know it is there in the long run, as you will take steps every day to become the person you want to be. Be patient with your mind as it veers off while you are trying to meditate. And be patient with your fears. Don't be embarrassed or ashamed of any of them, but gradually see them for what they are.

I meet many people who feel they could do so much more if they could just throw out their fears and anxieties. But rather than try to ignore fears, there is something to be said for looking into the heart of them, accepting them and then walking through them. If we can look at fears or worries from another angle, then we will often find something inspiring, something we truly want to do with our lives. For our fears are very much related to our hopes – we fear a negative outcome, just as we hope for the positive: someone who is afraid to get married also knows deep down the potential happiness from being in a loving, committed relationship with all the barriers from their past relationships dissolved; in exactly the same place where we imagine failure there is also the potential for success; and we fear losing the good things that we currently have, sometimes so much so that we forget to enjoy them.

If we decide sometimes to turn away from our fears and walk away, there should be no shame or regret, but also why not jump in and use them as our inspiration? They hold such potential for growth and often they are not nearly as scary as our imagination. This is why it is important to remember the changing nature of life – that we won't be able to control every little detail, and that we shouldn't even try to. If, for example, we were to try and control our partner out of a fear that they might outgrow our relationship then we are just stifling something really good in our lives that is meant to change and grow.

Let's think about the 'three things' again and whether any of the meditations may be of help with both facing and letting go of our fears. Remember that the only person who is truly the source of either your happiness or your suffering is you. How you choose to look at situations makes all the difference – with your mind you create your world. But of course, we can't control everything around us and the world is constantly uncertain and subject to change. And it is by accepting that uncertainty that we can decide to say, why not look on the bright side? Why not give things a go, even if we are a little afraid? I don't know anyone who regretted trying, even when things didn't turn out the way they had hoped or expected, as even 'failure' is something that can be looked at from a different point of view.

If we are practising the Appreciation and Contemplating Change meditations, we can build up our confidence in the face of our fears. We might realise that it is not worth spending all our time constantly turning over and thinking about our worries and fears, that we have a great many really good things in our lives that should be given greater mental prominence! And through the contemplation meditations we can learn to sit with our fears without being overwhelmed by them. We can keep a little mental distance and look at them from different angles. We can accept them and, in time, notice that we no longer grasp at them.

Most of the time, when we humans sit together and chit chat, we tend to find it very easy to complain or criticise. It's very rare that we sit there praising others, especially those we don't like. I think our ego takes up so much of the conversation that we forget to be daringly different, daringly positive, daringly kind and daringly understanding.

I always tell my friends and students, it's easy to complain because it makes our ego so happy, especially if we can bring others in on the act. We feed our ego to feel good fleetingly, but then we don't feel very good at all once the moment passes.

A hero is someone who is daring to live a happy life and who conquers their ego and controls those jealous, insecure or proud emotions that make us

do or say things that hurt others. So always check
yourself and try, daringly, to stop. It takes a lot
of courage to admit we are wrong and that we
need to change and improve. It's okay to make
mistakes, but it takes courage to learn from them,
to wish to be a better person. With a willingness to
improve, you will be walking your path, little by
little. One day, without even noticing, you will
become a great and kind person.
His Holiness Gyalwang Drukpa

Letting go of attitudes

When a man bows, heaven forgives.
Tibetan proverb

As humans, we are lucky enough to have five or perhaps even six senses through which we take in the world around us. But despite this, it seems that we can sometimes tend towards developing fixed attitudes rather than staying open to what each day or moment might bring. We become stuck in old patterns and ways of thinking, which at first might seem easier and more comfortable than always having to try to see everyone else's point of view. But the trouble is that the mind becomes like a closed box, and new ideas just pour off the sides because we feel our minds are already full.

With this rigid outlook we might also develop a sense of either arrogance or fussiness, even fanaticism. We tend to associate the word 'ego' with arrogance;

people we describe as having a big ego are usually the loudest and the pushiest, while we associate quiet with more humility. But the ego can be just as strong in a quiet, even very sensitive person. You see, if we take everything extremely personally, then it is the ego taking over once more, just as it is the ego that shouts and blusters in a very arrogant person. In both cases their pride is very easily pricked, causing one to go on the attack while the other feels cut to the quick.

There are many people who seem calm on the outside, but who are made restless in their minds by the impossible quest to always be right, or perfect. The slightest criticism or joke pricks their sensitivity and they feel as though they might crumble inside. Things have to be just so, or else a sense of frustration or anxiety begins to bubble up, and there is such a strong sense of 'right' and 'wrong' that there is no room to move. And just as they take everything so much to heart, someone caught up in fussiness might also be very judgemental of others. The mind doesn't have a natural ebb and flow, but often feels as though it is always coming up against obstacles, pointing out the weaknesses in others while feeling so sensitive about their own.

You are right

Two monks came out of a lecture and entered into a debate over what they had heard. Each of them insisted that his understanding was the correct one. To settle the dispute, they went to see the master for a judgement.

After hearing the argument put forward by the first monk, the master said, 'You are right!' At this, the monk was very happy. Casting a winner's glance at his friend, he left the room.

The second monk became upset and started to put his own ideas to the master about what he understood from the lecture. After he finished, the master looked at him and said, 'You are right too.' Hearing this, the second monk brightened up and went away.

A third monk who was also in the room was greatly puzzled by what he saw. He said, 'I am confused, master! Their positions regarding the issue are completely opposite. They can't be both right!'

The master smiled as he looked into the eyes of this third monk and said, 'You are also right!'

And then there is fanaticism, and it is something we are all too aware of in Buddhism. My guru the 12th Gyalwang Drukpa likes to talk of spirituality and not religion because he is so aware of how fanaticism can creep in, even when we start with the best intentions. It is such a shame that religion can be taken to fanatical extremes, to the point where people will even kill others in the name of their faith. On a milder note, we try not to focus too much on the rituals of Buddhism within our own teachings as they can overtake the reasons for being spiritual in the first place. It is easy to get caught up in saying the prayers 100 per cent correctly, rather than focusing on what they mean.

Finding comfort in the ritual of one's day or one's faith is not a bad thing at all. There is no set dividing line between what is good or helpful and what is bad or unhelpful, no universal definition. And so all I try to encourage is that you, as an individual, find the place where you feel more relaxed and comfortable in your mind. When you feel fussiness coming, try to take a step away from yourself and take a look at your thoughts as they tighten and become unhappy. Begin to see your fussiness for what it is – something that doesn't need to grip your mind so tightly. Flexibility is so important to a happy mind. Don't be so quick to criticise, to argue or disagree. Leave things be. Do things in a way that is comfortable for you, but don't be nosy about how others are doing things. Thinking or speaking badly of others is a source of so much negativity in the world. Let us instead concentrate on investigating ourselves with an open heart to the world.

Letting go of praise and blame

As we make our way through life, we do like to receive feedback from those around us and, in particular, we like to get the odd pat on the back. It's completely natural to be happy when others are pleased with our actions; the mental skill here is in not becoming overly attached to that praise, so that we start to need it for our sense of self-worth. Because then, when it is taken away, we feel lost without it and our confidence takes a nose dive. So if you have done something very good and people are praising you, appreciate it and give thanks. But do not become attached to the praise; do not let it feed your sense of pride.

As for blame, you need not become attached to it either, whether it has been directed at you or people are trying to apportion blame somehow in the fallout of a particular situation. If you feel you are in the firing line, you might want to gently investigate, but do so in a way that is always kind to yourself. Taking blame to heart can put us off track for much longer than is needed to learn the lesson; it can really take root in the mind and feed any negative feelings we have about ourselves. This is why the Appreciation meditation is so helpful when it comes to the daily ups and downs of life. By focusing first on the things that you are very thankful for in your life, you can then explore issues like blame without getting dragged down into negative thoughts. You might decide there is something you can learn and therefore do differently in future, in which case, go ahead and do it. Otherwise, if there is nothing you can do about it, then that's the bottom line, and worrying won't change matters. It will never make things better.

When we are very sensitive to either praise and blame, or both, and criticism too, we tend to place rather too much importance on our own actions, and this makes us vulnerable to the restless mind. The relentless search for perfection is exhausting. You might be a very conscientious person, for whom every task carries so much weight and just a hint of not being top of the class or of letting other people down means that you can never let up; if so, at some point you will end up very disappointed in yourself, despite your amazing efforts.

So if we can loosen our attachment to praise and blame, we can stay balanced in our emotions either way. When we recognise that none of us is perfect a great weight lifts from our shoulders. We are often less fussy with ourselves and others and we give ourselves the opportunity to improve and grow. Life opens up and we feel less fear and anxiety, less pressure to get everything right, relaxed in the knowledge that, come what may, we will try our best.

Use generosity to let go

Whatever it is that you grasp on to in life, as you read through this book I encourage you to gently loosen that grasp and lighten your mental and emotional load a little.

Whatever it is you are attached to, find a way to offer it, even if only in your mind. The simplest example might be money. If you are very attached to money, then practise giving away just a little (this is not about grand gestures), and do so from the depths of your heart, with no conditions or strings attached. If someone were very jealous of a friend or colleague they might practise celebrating the efforts of that person instead, so offering good feelings instead of negative. You might need to think creatively, but explore all the ways in which you can give instead of holding on.

Letting go of negative influences

There are some things or people in our lives that we know deep down just aren't very good for us. Sometimes these are the things or people we most desire, or those who are an intrinsic part of our lives – our family, for example, or our colleagues. You might think that being more accepting of the impermanence of life and its ups and downs equates with always having to be stoic about situations or people that we do not get on with – that we should learn how to 'put up' with them and be less complaining or negative in our thoughts about them. But if we learn to heighten our self-awareness through some of the practices included in this book, we begin to understand that there are times when it is actually more healthy to remove ourselves from the negative influences of certain situations, things or people and concentrate instead on nurturing those influences we know in our heart to be good for us.

There are times when you just have to take a deep breath and acknowledge a negative influence to be just that – you can't fix it or change it. For example, you might have a very difficult relationship with your boss, but you very much want to stay in your job for many other reasons. The act of acceptance and recognition might be enough to take the sting out of this negative relationship.

Occasionally, you might need to actively let something or someone go, because these negative influences can wreak havoc on the restful mind. We can become fixated on them, thinking constantly about things that are not good for our peace of mind or happiness. This person might even be very close to you, like a family member or partner. Despite all your efforts to have a positive relationship, you realise that it is having a negative impact on your life and your mind. You might think it selfish or weak to give something up, rather than stay around and cope with whatever comes your way, but actually sometimes the strongest moments of our lives are when we are taking ourselves out of a negative cycle or pattern, because that is when we truly make a change for the better.

Coming Back to the Present

The secret of health for both mind and body is not to mourn for the past, worry about the future, or anticipate troubles, but to live in the present moment wisely and earnestly.
Buddha

Many of us in today's developed world are lucky enough to have good relationships either with family, friends or loved ones, a roof over our heads, food to eat and the basics of warmth and shelter. There are still people throughout the world though who do not even have these basics of life.

I think it is at the point where we feel truly happy to have a hot meal or a warm fire that we learn the great lesson of living in the present, content to be right here and nowhere else. It isn't always so easy. At the fast pace of modern living, with all the technology we have at our fingertips, twenty-four hours a day, it isn't always easy to remember this. But for me, nature is one the biggest reminders of how to be present, hence the tradition of the *Pad Yatra*, the walking pilgrimage.

The walk

The *Pad Yatra* is a forty-two-day walking pilgrimage undertaken by 700 nuns and volunteers trekking across the Himalayas with a call to spread the message of ecological compassion throughout the region. This is a cause very dear to my own heart and to that of His Holiness the Gyalwang Drukpa. The mountains of the Himalayas are not only a sacred place for us, where a great many people live the Buddhist philosophy, but they are also an environmentally sacred place for the entire world, a glacial region that is in danger of being devastated by the climate chaos associated with global warming.

We trekked together on foot for the forty-two days, from village to village, picking up half a ton of plastic rubbish along the way, strapped to our backs. We talked to many people along the way and were greeted with immense kindness and generosity of spirit. But I must admit it was not a fun experience at first, and I would like to share with you many questions that came up in my own mind during that month and a half in the mountains. These were questions about purpose, about happiness, suffering and the meaning of life.

Things were not very easy, especially at the beginning. There was no shower, no bathroom, not much to eat and we slept in tents. All we did was walk, walk and walk.

There was a joke among the Ladakhis about one mountain – that when you looked at the top of it, your head would fall off. That's how steep it was. So what we did was to set goals for ourselves. We would not look up for five minutes then, when we reached a certain point, instead of looking up and feeling tired, we would look down and we'd think: 'Wow, we have done quite a lot this time.' In this way, step by step, we would accumulate happiness, slowly crossing this kind of mountain – of which there were many – and gradually finding enjoyment in our achievement.

After a while, despite the lack of food, sleep and basic necessities, I found that I was enjoying the walk. I asked myself why? When I looked at my own experiences, I realised that there were many reasons, but one of them was that I was living in the moment, living in the present and just concentrating on the walking – putting one foot in front of the other, one step at a time. It was a case of just concentrating on the moment because to lose concentration meant danger. It became quite simple. And there was all that natural beauty surrounding us, right there – we couldn't miss it because it wouldn't let us.

Some of the Western volunteers on the walk were really struggling though. They were caught up either in their suffering as they found the walking so tough on their bodies, or they were so focused on the top of the mountain that they were missing out on the beautiful journey to get there. But then one day something changed. They stopped looking so far ahead and instead started, like me, to just put one foot in front of the other. Suddenly, there were smiles where there had been tears and exhaustion. Worries about whether they might make it lost their grip and a pure enjoyment of the present moment came instead.

So my question is: when you live, do you really enjoy

the present? Are you in the present and are you aware of the present?

The fact is we all want to enjoy life. But some of us believe that enjoying life is related to the future somehow, about 'happiness of the becoming', while others feel very nostalgic about a time in their past, when they believe things were just the way they wanted them to be. If you think about it, though, the present moment in which we are living, why shouldn't we also appreciate it? What do we really have in this life except the present? So why not enjoy this moment and the life that is going to become the future at the same time. Why not think fondly of the past, but also revel in the sensory experience of the present. There really is no time like the present to start appreciating our life.

The second interesting point about the *Pad Yatra* relates to food. During the walk, everything we ate tasted delicious because we were hungry. It was not comparable to any food we would usually choose to eat in our everyday lives, but back then it tasted better than the food in the top restaurants in Hong Kong. Similarly, while we might be used to sleeping in comfortable beds most of the time, the sleeping bag in the tent felt wonderful and we slept so deeply because we were exhausted. We were always so happy to see our sleeping bags. We were happy with the simple life we were living!

So while the *Pad Yatra* is invaluable in bringing help to remote parts of the world, it is also like going to a gym for the mind. For me, it was like tightening my belt both physically and mentally!

Simplicity brings us back into the present

I have just three things to teach: simplicity, patience, compassion. These three are your greatest treasures.
Lao Tzu

Modern life can sometimes become rather complex. We have so many choices to make, so many emails to read, let alone answer. You might be sitting in one meeting thinking about the next, or how you're going to leave on time to pick up your children from school. You might be in a gallery, wandering through an exhibition you've been wanting to see for months, then find yourself thinking about other things that have been playing on your mind. If this is ever the case, then the breathing exercise on p. 89 will help to bring you back into the present, as it brings you back into your body. Just centring your breath and drawing it in deeper into yourself will help your mind to be less of a time traveller.

Begin to be aware of any opportunities to simplify your life. It might start with taking half an hour each lunchtime to actually switch off or be away from the computer so that you can have a little time just to eat, without trying to do lots of other things simultaneously. Here are some other ideas:

- Spend a day doing each little thing with your mind fully engaged, from brushing your teeth to making a pot of tea. You are practising bringing your mind into the present moment. It might seem a little contrived to begin with, but you will be surprised at how you begin to enjoy the smallest trivia in the day, even the washing up!

- If you feel the burn of irritation triggered by an everyday situation that just seems to push your buttons, a very good way to distract your mind from the irritation and ease the rising tension is to come back into the present and focus on your breath. It might have started to become a little shallow, so you can gently begin to draw deeper breaths right down into your stomach. Don't be tempted to heave a huge sigh – a sure sign not only to you but to the world that you are agitated and frustrated about something. Keep your breaths quiet and slow and, as you breathe in, imagine that white light (see p. 93). You might also find a moment of appreciation is a helpful way to diffuse restless emotions or to distract your mind so that the irritation is prevented from growing into something more unpleasant. If you can train your mind to do something else, then you will be more likely to see the situation in a different light, and perhaps see that it might not be worth getting so worked up about. Even if you still feel that someone has acted rudely, that you have been slighted or that something unfair has happened, you are able to move on more quickly from the heat of the reaction. You no longer carry it with you for the rest of your day, so that it colours your mood and interactions with other people (none of whom knows what an unfortunate morning you might have had).

- Before you do anything that tends to make you feel nervous or stressed, focus on the breath to bring yourself away from the worry associated with what might happen, or what happened before, and into the present moment. Add a minute of Appreciation meditation (see p. 102) to lighten things up in your mind too. This can be very helpful if you are nervous about making or answering phone calls, travelling, giving presentations or going to see someone such as the doctor, dentist or head teacher, for example.
- See if you can find activities that allow you to *think* less, at least about the usual day-to-day things, and simply *be* more. Sports can be very helpful in this respect. Many golfers will spend four hours meditating on the course, focused on nothing but that small white ball. The same is true of painting, pottery, singing, climbing, horse riding. Any activity that helps

to focus your mind on something other than the usual mind chatter is like a vacation for the mind and usually helps bring you into the flow of the present moment.

- Practising your listening skills will help you to be truly present with the other people around you and is a very generous act too. When you find yourself finishing another person's sentence or wanting them to get to the end of their bit of the conversation so that you can say your piece, you are constantly jumping ahead in your mind, which can make you feel rather jumpy and agitated in yourself. Relax, let your mind quiet down and listen to someone else for a change.

When I gave a talk about the *Pad Yatra* and the many helpful lessons I felt it had taught me about enjoying the present, there were a few very interesting questions afterwards, and I thought I would include them here:

Q. If you have dreams or ambitions, does that mean you are not living in the present?

A. Having dreams and wanting to achieve is fine, but if you are always dreaming and never appreciating, enjoying or living in the present, then even if you fulfil your dreams, there will be no point. You will just make another dream, and if you live in one dream after another, without paying attention to what's around you in the here and now, you may end up dreaming alone.

Q. Can you use the past to help in the present?

A. Contemplating how we arrived at where we are is helpful for understanding our present. However, it is easy to become trapped in thinking about the past, and if we do that we are not finding any lessons for our current day. We may be nostalgic for something that has gone, or we may be holding on to hurts or grief. This is where we need to be brave enough to allow these emotions to come in our meditation so we may look at them, without judgement, neither rejecting them nor holding on to them, but seeing them a little more clearly for what they are and what they were. They are a part of us, but we are not them. Gently, we can let them fade. Gradually, we can allow ourselves to be more fully in the present, to find our happiness in everything that is around us today.

Q. What if you feel stuck in the present?

A. Some people have a sense that they want to escape their present – that it is all very well to say live in and enjoy the present, but that it isn't so easy when you are in a job you hate or a relationship you can't find a way out of. You might feel trapped by your 'present' circumstances. The problem, and therefore the answer to this might be found not externally, but internally. Does the problem lie with the job, relationship or financial situation, or is it related to our projected expectations and standards? Even in dream jobs and dream relationships, don't we sometimes wonder whether we are happy? We tell ourselves we should be happy – that we have everything we could possibly want or need – and yet somehow we are not happy. I think there are nearly always positive things in our life at *any* point, but usually we fail to see these in the moment; we may not even realise until we have lost them. This is why the Appreciation and Contemplating Change meditations (see pp. 102 and 107 respectively) combined are crucial for the relaxed and restful mind.

If we give ourselves just a little time, even a few minutes, to contemplate each day, then we become more observant, more understanding of ourselves and others, less quick to judge and make assumptions and more appreciative of the moment and the task we are doing right now. With appreciation comes happiness, rather than always waiting for that elusive something which will then lay happiness at our feet. Why not be happy *right now*?

Nourishing the Body to Nourish the Mind

Your body and mind are, as we have seen, very much interdependent. An awareness of your body comes from the mind; if you listen to your body, you will be able to take better care of yourself. And if you take care of your body, you are also taking great steps to take care of your mind.

To understand just how close the connection is between body and mind, think for a moment of a smile versus a frown. The choice you make will have an immediate effect on your mind. When you frown you create those two deep furrows between your eyes – you might say you even close up your third eye, the gateway to your inner wisdom. Your face feels tense and your mind follows, becoming rigid and uncomfortable.

But when you smile, everything opens up, including your mind. People are drawn to your eyes, the good feelings are contagious. You just feel better. No wonder they say that laughter is the best medicine.

In meditation, we connect with the breath to give our minds a chance to rest. Just stopping the flow of negative or rushing thoughts, even if only for a minute, allows us to regenerate and reinvigorate our mental energy.

Walking meditation

To walk: such a simple thing and yet what better way to ground us, to connect. To take a step in life is to live life; to walk one's path. A walking meditation might be a time for inner observing, but often it helps us to connect outwards too, providing a balance between the two. We connect with our bodies, bringing the physical self closer to the inner self, so it's like an active form of retreat. And we connect with our environment – again, bringing the physical nature closer to our inner self. We can observe our emotional state, using the rhythm of our steps and our breathing to slow things down and see what's happening in our minds today.

When walking on the *Pad Yatra* (see p. 156) we fell into a rhythm of literally just putting one foot in front of the next. The path could be very steep and treacherous, so we became acutely aware of our bodies. For many of the participants it was so physically challenging that they finally let go of their restless minds and a look of great joy suddenly came over them as they experienced life in the moment.

While on retreat we will often 'circumambulate', which simply means walking for many circuits around the 'stupa' (a structure that contains Buddhist relics). This type of walking helps to give our egos a break as we dissolve into the rhythm of our steps. Sometimes we will meditate as we go around, or just let our minds settle, or we might chat quietly with our friends, catching up and discussing the ideas we heard during the day's teaching. Just focusing on counting how many times we have made the circuit can be enough to give our minds a break, or we can use the time to contemplate. It can be whatever we need it to be.

Getting started

You can do a few minutes of walking meditation at any time of the day, whether you are in the park or even along a city street. To practise though, it may be a good idea to go somewhere a little more quiet and natural as you will be less easily distracted. Try to find somewhere with uneven ground, then you will be truly present in your walking, rather than constantly drifting back to your busy life.

- Before you begin, simply stand for a few moments. Feel the connection between your feet and the ground and then upwards through your body, up and out of the top of your head. Relax your shoulders, don't let your knees lock and look directly ahead. Relax your jaw, your eyes, your forehead. Take in the moment.
- Breathe gently from your belly, and feel this as the centre of your body (so often we are caught up in our heads as the centre of our being).
- Breathe deeply, taking time on the exhale. Just put one foot in front of the other and enjoy each step. Appreciate your body as you move. Appreciate the earth beneath your feet, feel

the sensations between the two and throughout your body.

- Keep your focus gently ahead and begin to sense your emotional state, just observing, not trying to fix anything. Is your mind racing all over the place or is it calm and enjoying a meander? Let your thoughts come and go with the rhythm of your pace, your breath.

- Feel the breeze on your face. Just allow nature to infuse your body. Feel the release each time your foot leaves the ground, and the connection as you meet it.

- After a few minutes, building up over time if you like, gently come to a stop and spend a few moments just standing again, feeling the ground beneath your feet, sensing your body and mind.

You might fall into meditative walking as you go about your day – a little rest and recharge for the mind. Or you might prefer to dedicate a little time for this practice, which is certainly a very good way to begin.

Feed your mind

Just as food is energy for our body, it is energy for our mind. And it turns out that there are foods that are especially beneficial to a calm, focused and healthy mind. We know that a good breakfast helps children to concentrate better at school, yet so many adults rush out of the door in the morning without giving their minds any good fuel to get through the day. Then, by mid-afternoon they feel frayed, running on empty.

Scientists have even identified some of the nutrients that are particularly good for the mind, and at the top of the list come the omega 3 essential fatty acids, which help the emotional part of the brain to increase production of the neurotransmitters associated with positive mood. Flaxseeds are full of these omega 3s.

Eating mindfully

At a retreat near Kathmandu in Nepal, where many of our visitors were from Vietnam, the food was a wonderful combination of Nepalese and Vietnamese dishes and, despite the remote location, no two meals were the same during the entire week. What is very good to see on the retreats, as on the *Pad Yatras*, is how mindful people are of the food they are eating. They are mindful of taking just enough to satisfy their appetites and they seem to savour every mouthful. Often we are encouraged to eat in silence, reminding us to appreciate and simply eat to eat.

The food is always simple (we are vegetarians because we do not believe in harming any beings), but it is prepared with care and the nuns will make use of every ingredient they have to hand. Of course, rice is a staple; it is one of those basic foods that always brings us back to simplicity, while reminding us of how precious food is. With the vast array of foods available in supermarkets, restaurants and vending machines in even the most bizarre places, sometimes a simple bowl of rice and vegetables is all we need to bring ourselves back into our minds and appreciate life: if we have rice, we'll be ok. We also drink hot water and traditional tea throughout the retreats – again, very simple, but much appreciated. And it is so good to see people serving each other with big smiles after a day of meditation and teaching.

Fasting is something that we do on particular days according to the Tibetan calendar. If a fast day falls during the retreat, participants are encouraged to fast for the second half of the day if they wish to. Again, this highlights the relationship between body and mind, giving our bodies a rest for a short time.

Before I first went on *Pad Yatra* with His Holiness I was very fussy about food and about what I did and didn't like to eat. But on the walking pilgrimage through the mountains we never knew where we were going to be able to stop from day to day, so we never knew what food there would be to eat. I soon discovered that real hunger makes a meal of potatoes taste like they have never tasted before.

In mindfulness programmes, food or tea are often used to engage all the senses with the mind, to encourage more awareness of how they smell, look, feel and taste. They might suggest taking a piece of chocolate and observing closely everything about it as it dissolves in the mouth. It's a little like the Daily Breathing meditation in that we bring our attention away from the restlessness of our minds to something more immediate and physical. And if we can practise this kind of mindful eating every once in a while, then it will have the gentle knock-on effect of helping us to be more aware of the little, but vital things in our days – from the sun on our face to a cup of tea – all of which can help us to cultivate a restful mind and give us a little piece of joy.

Exercise your mind

Along with eating well for the mind, exercise is definitely very good for it too. It doesn't matter how you choose to exercise. For example, I love the 'mind gym' of the *Pad Yatra* (page 156), the walking pilgrimages we take through the Himalayas. Whether you like to run, swim, bicycle (we do cycling *Pad Yatras* too!) anything you can do to train your physical body will also help to train your mind. When you are exercising your body you often give your mind a nice rest, at least from all the restless worries. Even if you have to concentrate quite a bit on your chosen exercise, like working out your next shot in golf or tennis, you are using your mind in a different way; you're even exercising your mind at the same time as your body.

This is certainly the case with yoga, which has always

been closely associated with meditation. In fact, we even see yoga as the physical form of meditation: just as meditation opens up your mind and allows it to stretch, recuperate and find new ways in which to grow, so yoga does the same for your body.

Yoga is all about balance. It might seem as though you are not moving all that much during a yoga class, but then afterwards you feel as if your whole body has been stretched in ways you never knew it could be. Some practitioners even say that you can tell how your mind is doing through the way your body is in yoga. If one day you feel much more off balance than usual, you might be feeling the same way in your thoughts or emotions.

Along with balance there is also flexibility, so that you can be firmly rooted like a tree and yet sway in the breeze with ease and without the fear of falling down. This is exactly what meditation aims to do for the mind: to restore balance and flexibility, so that we can feel strong, but also adaptable to whatever may come our way.

3

Everyday Mindfulness

Tell me and I'll forget; show me and I may remember;
involve me and I'll understand.
Chinese proverb

From drinking a cup of coffee to caring for your loved
ones, being in your life adds colour and richness.

When we are mindful we're both spontaneous and
well prepared because with a little more understanding
and knowledge of our minds we can act more intui-
tively: we can speak up more often, while being aware
of our words; we can immerse ourselves in whatever
we are doing, no longer anxious about the outcome
because we are confident in the intention; and we are
fully present in the moment and in our own minds and
bodies, rather than constantly disappearing into the
past or future of our minds.

This section explores some very specific situations

in life and how the restful mind might offer a helpful approach.

Many people think we Buddhists are only about being and never doing, but it's really that we need to be before we can do: we need to understand who we are, and then we strive to get a great deal done, driven by love and compassion, rather than our selfish agenda. When we have understanding we remember what inspires us – why we do what we do. Inspiration then gives us momentum – it is our energy and something very special. We are no longer following our dreams, always one step behind, but *being* them, from moment to moment, day to day.

Experience is the best practice. It is the best lesson. How can we really learn or understand without experience? That is why I always encourage people not to be afraid to try, because if you try your best, you will have a great experience. Often, it is easier to look at other people's lives than your own, to desire someone else's day. But you just end up missing out and getting lost in what-ifs, rather than being present in your life here and now, which is all you ever have.

Daily Habits of the Restful Mind

You might not realise that you already have many ways to help calm your own restless mind. The trouble is that it's easy to get fixated on what you are doing wrong, rather than cultivating what you are doing right.

As you read through this section, you might think of some of the suggestions as luxuries rather than essentials, but if you can keep your mind nourished and restful, then you can go through your day with so much more energy and freedom. You will be open to the opportunities that come your way, and more resilient when things don't go so well or according to your plans or hopes. You will be an easier person for others to get on with, and find your own irritations tend to come and go more swiftly too, rather than hanging around and ruining everyone's day.

As we saw in the first part of the book, it's easy to fall into a way of thinking that equates success or some kind of achievement with happiness – the type of happiness that requires conditions, hurdles we have to jump over to reach it. For example, if I make so many sales today, then I will be happy. The trouble is that although such things might be well worth aiming for, if we rely on them for our happiness, then it will always tend to be fleeting, rather than sustained, when actually, we are able to nourish and cultivate happiness and peace in our minds often through smaller everyday habits.

These habits will help you to keep in mind the bigger picture of your life, even when things get difficult. Use them to bring you back into the present, away from worries about things that have been or may or may not happen. Whether it is a walk by the river or pumping weights at the gym that gives you peace of mind, think about how these things make you feel good and relaxed, and what you can do to bring that sense of contentment into more of your day.

Breathe

Awareness of body and breath is the first step towards awareness of your emotions and reactions in everyday situations. If you sense that your body is tensing up, then it is likely your mind will soon follow. Try to focus on your breath, on the in and the out, to allow your mind a chance to pause. Draw your breath deep into your body. You might still react to the situation, but with more awareness and, it is likely, in a calmer, more patient way. The Daily Breathing exercise (see p. 89) will bring you back into your body and give your mind a rest and a feeling of spaciousness. It creates a small gap between you and whatever difficult or frustrating situation you are facing. It gives you a chance to pause before you react, and a chance to think before you speak. You can also use this practice to help calm anxiety before doing something that tends to make you feel nervous, like making a phone call, visiting the doctor or dentist, or stepping on to a busy train.

Choose your words wisely

Better than a thousand hollow words, is one word that brings peace.
Buddha

It will help your own peace of mind to mean everything you say from the depths of your heart. As Buddha said, 'Better than a thousand hollow words, is one that brings peace.' Words give us an opportunity to connect with others, to show compassion and share creativity and ideas. But they can also hurt people; they can be critical and blaming of others, they can be bullying or gossipy or they can exaggerate our pain and suffering.

Often when a person is very critical of others, they are projecting their own inner critic, the loudest critic of all. Or perhaps it is the 'I-am-best' part of the ego that is coming to the surface. This isn't to say one should never utter a word of criticism, but always be aware of where it is coming from. If it is given with generosity, love and kindness, and of course if you are in the role of teacher or mentor, then you will do this often in your position and you will know which words will be helpful to another in learning and growing as a person.

Always bring yourself back into the present when you speak – *be* with your words. In this way, you will truly mean what you say, rather than throwing out words while your thoughts are elsewhere. A parent, for example, may be kind yet firm with their child who is being naughty. They don't shout or even raise their voice, but they are fully present with their child and their words, and their child always knows when they mean it. I think as adults we do too, but we just have so many more layers that have built up over time. We use jargon, stock words and phrases without really thinking about them. But we still know when a politician who is delivering the lines of a speech cares deeply about what they are saying, or when they could be just as emotional about reading out a shopping list. We know when our lover pauses to really feel those words, 'I love you,' or if they are just saying them out of habit. And even if we bristle and squirm, we know when words of criticism are meant to help us.

By bringing your awareness back into your words you will see the difference it makes in all of your relationships and so many moments in the day.

The gift of silence

Watch one's own mind as it is definitely the guru.
Milarepa

If we are able to keep silent for even one hour in a day, we can really begin to develop our insight and restful mind. We often waste time with gossip, talking of others, and this wastes energy too. So instead of always talking, always looking outside ourselves, take the opportunity of silence to look inside. Don't be afraid of the quiet; don't be afraid of sitting still. It is in these moments that your inner self will stretch and grow, and so external life will naturally improve too without worrying about it so much.

Taking yourself away from all the stimulation, input and distractions of your daily life every now and then can help you in learning to release attachments to lots of things. When people come to our retreats they wear very simple, warm clothing and the shower is just a bucket of hot water and a cup. There are no cars and we encourage everyone to turn off their phones and BlackBerries. For some people there is instant welcome relief, while for others this 'switching off' can take a bit of getting used to. But when the trappings of modern-day living are no longer there as distractions, it's amazing how quickly people begin to see beneath the layers of the restless ego mind to their inner nature.

Chit-chat is something people love to do as a release from the stresses and strains of daily life, but while in the environment of the retreat we encourage people to be quiet and still, to give their minds a chance to breathe and open up. Some retreats are completely silent, but for beginners especially we like to encourage people to explore the teachings with each other a little, and then have their own time to contemplate. You can do this in your own life, whether at a formal meditation session if that is right for you, or simply by getting back to nature once in a while for a walk in the country, carrying your lunch on your back.

If you can practise not speaking, you might find that you become less inclined towards angry or emotional speech. This isn't about becoming a pushover, but you will begin to recognise the times when you wish you could take something you said back, and stop yourself before it's too late to do so.

Read, look, listen

When we are very busy we might find that we go for long periods without reading, listening to music or taking in art or culture. We can't seem to find the room in our minds or the time in our schedule. And yet, when we do pick up a book and read just a few pages, we feel our minds expand. We feel less stuck when we are not seeing and thinking about everything from only our own point of view. We see through the writer's or painter's imagination. We remind ourselves how good it is just to listen, whether to music or even the birds in the garden. This is very helpful as we go about our own lives with the people closest to us. We might not always agree with the views of others, but it is still a very good practice to be less fixed in our own – to be able to listen without wanting to interrupt. Taking in culture helps us to open up and broaden out our minds, giving us lots of room to grow within ourselves and to be interested in others.

Give thanks

The Appreciation meditation combined with the Contemplating Change meditation (see pp. 102 and 107 respectively), is an excellent way to stop restlessness in the mind from taking hold. As you give thanks for everything good and supportive in your life you find that your own love and compassion will multiply. You will begin to be able to see the things that make you restless for what they are; they are things that don't have to take root, and it's up to you whether you let them take up precious room in your mind or whether you concentrate on the good in your life instead. Appreciation helps us to put things into perspective: we are reminded of the things that really matter, and can even use the positive emotions it creates to draw lessons from a day that hasn't gone so well because, on balance, we still feel very lucky and are able to find things to be thankful for.

Change a habit

In everyday life people have a lot of ingrained habits that are perfectly harmless, but encourage the mind to do as much as possible on autopilot. So from the route you take to work, to the café where you get your morning coffee or where you sit in meetings, you might follow the same pattern every day. Changing one of these habits can be very refreshing for the mind as it brings you back into the present, so you might see things a little differently and enjoy the change. You'll begin to feed your curiosity, and you never know what you might discover. A simple exercise like this can really heighten your awareness of how you react to certain situations in the same way each time, and show you that habits can be broken.

Changing an automatic behaviour can also be light relief from focusing too much on working on the mind. I realise that this book encourages you to get to know your mind, and there is the danger of becoming rather too introspective and self-analytical. I think people are always surprised at how often myself and my teachers are laughing at ourselves, especially when we are being too serious, and the funny moments in life. I think if we can make a conscious effort to take care of our minds during specific practices then it releases us from too much introspection for the rest of the day to get on with living in the moment.

What went well today?

Why not spend a little time dwelling on what you did well today? Put aside your worries about all the things still left on your to-do list and let yourself feel good about what you did. Like the Appreciation meditation, this habit is about perspective. It's about training the mind to see that glass as half full rather than half empty.

Asking ourselves how our day went is an automatic cue for most of us, as we like to evaluate how things are going. And yet often we then launch into a list of criticisms, afraid that dwelling on the good things is big-headed and complacent. But whether you are someone who tends to be self-critical or you are at the other end of the scale and sweep anything negative straight under the carpet without a second glance, try to be balanced in how you look at your day. Use the things that went well to boost your confidence and help you relax during your evening.

Doing your best

This is a daily habit that we are often very good at instilling in our children, but which we may place less value on as we get older and start judging how successful we are by comparing ourselves to others. But doing your best today, right here in the present, *is* the restful mind. It isn't about worrying how good you are, or looking across the room at others all the time or putting a label on yourself. It is about cutting out all of the usual mind clutter and doing what you do, with your best intentions and your best efforts.

It's so easy to spend all day worrying about one thing, but not actually do it. Everything else then gets put off and you feel like you've wasted a day, while your fear has grown and taken root like some kind of scary monster in your mind, making it even harder to get on with it. So if there is something on your to-do list that makes you anxious, try making it the first thing you do in your day, then you can relax and enjoy the rest of the day. Usually it goes just fine anyway, as it is your mind that has got carried away and imagined the worst-case scenario.

Eat well

A smiling face is half the meal.
Latvian proverb

Many people will grab lunch at their desks, standing up in the kitchen or even walking along the street. Eating has become another thing on our to-do list – something we can do at the same time as running errands, answering emails or surfing the web.

Yet food is a gift; it gives us life, and if you give a little time and thought to eating, then your body and mind will reap even more benefits. Sitting together with your family or just on your own quietly, savouring every mouthful, makes a meal so much more nourishing than just the food you eat. Food is a source of great joy for many – even a cup of tea can provide the perfect break for your mind during a busy day (see 'Feed your mind', p. 169).

Go for a walk

The Walking meditation (see p. 166) or simply going for a walk is one of the easiest ways to ease the restless mind. Even if you tend to think through things, rather than stop thinking as you walk, the energy flowing around your body and the rhythm of the movement will begin to help you settle. For some, a walk is a chance to leave the phone or the BlackBerry at home, and have a bit of time either with nature or just watching the world go by as you wander through the city streets.

Being with nature

If we spend time with nature, then we get to know our own nature a little better too. Nature has the ability to bring us back into the present as we catch sight of a rare bird or stand in awe of a view we have just climbed to. On the *Pad Yatra* (the walking pilgrimage – see p. 156) our main aim is to spread a message of eco-friendliness because, perhaps, if we can practise being friendly with nature, we can be friendly with and respectful towards each other too. Nature can be cruel and even violent, but also offers us so many gifts, especially for the restful mind – whether it is learning the lesson of taking one step at a time on the steep paths of the Himalayas or breathing in a place of calm as respite from the bustle of the city, we are so lucky to have her.

Laughing like nobody's business

My teacher His Holiness Gyalwang Drukpa uses this phrase, and what a sense of freedom and lightness there is in his words. Up on Druk Amitabha Mountain, in the Nepalese monastery for the Drukpa order of nuns, the nuns work so hard every day, looking after every aspect of the monastery, praying for many hours, then studying and doing physical activities like kung fu. It's certainly not an easy life, and yet you will always hear laughter coming from one corner or another of the monastery. There is always time for laughing like nobody's business.

When we start to contemplate our minds and our sense of self there is a danger of becoming too serious about it. In the search for happiness we forget to just have fun. Life is so precious, and yet we often put a sense of enjoyment very low down on our to-do list. We forget that it is when we are really enjoying ourselves the light shines through our eyes and lights up the hearts of others. Laughter is a great healer and connector of people. It is something very special that we have as human beings, and I think the restful mind is a mind that often sees the funny side of things. We can genuinely laugh at ourselves without putting ourselves down in any way.

If your heart has laughter in it, your mind feels happy. Laughter helps us through the sad times, offering a bit of light in through a darker part of life. So laugh like nobody's business!

Share your worries

Many people think it is selfish to talk of their worries and concerns; that really they have nothing to complain about and should just keep a lid on it. But if you can work on being a good listener to others, then others will, in turn, be helpful listeners to you when you need some care and support. Sharing a worry means sharing the burden, opening up a space within your mind so that you can take a breath and perhaps see and feel a concern in a less harsh light. Sometimes just talking things through is all you need because there isn't always a solution to your worry, and it's more a case of airing it to let it go. Don't bottle things up where they can become deep-seated and really upset your mind; when you bring them out in the open you might well find you can look at them from a new perspective, so that they no longer cause your mind to run wild.

Practise compassion

When you turn on the news today you would be forgiven for thinking there is little joy or happiness in the world and much suffering. But the constant barrage of bad news can have the effect of desensitising us to the suffering of others, as we feel helpless and wonder how one person can make any difference at all. For example, we think: how can we help every homeless person we come across? And so we just keep our heads down and walk past. We don't feel good about this though; it makes us uneasy and, deep down, we wish we could help in some way.

It is not comfortable feeling the suffering of others,

but if you can allow yourself to feel this pain, you are getting in touch with something at the very core of your inner nature, and that is your compassion.

Share your love and kindness

Practise giving every day – from giving a compliment, if you tend towards being critical, to giving change to a homeless person, if you know what it feels like to be a little grasping towards money or success. To practise giving unconditionally, even in just the smallest of ways, is very beneficial to the mind. It is a practice in loosening up and letting go. It's a cliché, but it's true, that the more kindness we give, the more we will open ourselves up to kindness in return.

If you notice something that brings you happiness in your day, share it with others.

Release any frustrations of the day

There is a saying, 'Don't let the sun go down on an argument', and the same is true of any negative feelings you have had during the day. This is why spending a few minutes in contemplation is so helpful, as you can acknowledge any difficulties that came up during the day and how you felt as you reacted. Then you can consider that you don't need to hold on to that negative feeling. You may yet have to address the situation, but you don't need to carry negative emotions to bed with you or get up with them in the morning. Don't dismiss the pain, but realise that it doesn't have to stay fixed in your mind; you have the choice to let it go.

Sleep

Someone once asked a Zen Master, 'How do you practise Zen?'

The master said, 'When you are hungry, eat; when you are tired, sleep.'

'Isn't that what everyone does anyway?'

The master replied, 'No, No. Most people entertain a thousand desires when they eat and scheme over a thousand plans when they sleep.'

A good night's sleep is an incredibly restorative tonic for the mind. When tired, the mind easily becomes stressed and tense, unfocused and unsure of which direction to take or choice to make. Don't be too hard on your mind when you are tired; allow yourself to rest and restore. If you tend to wake up in the early hours with a restless mind, churning things over and over, try to give yourself time to meditate during the day. This will encourage your mind to be more settled.

I am always amazed that so many people struggle with sleep when they have such busy days and their minds really need a break. But if we allow the mind to wander all over the place all day, then it's difficult to just switch it off when we want to go to sleep. In the quiet of the night, the same worries, fears, criticisms and constant attempts at problem-solving or list-making will come to the fore, often getting louder and louder.

Just as it is good to eat mindfully more often, it is sensible to go to sleep more mindfully too. For some, this means creating a ritual before going to bed to help slow down the mind and signal to the body that sleep is near – like drinking a soothing cup of tea or taking a hot bath. For others, exercising more and earlier in the day is a great way to induce more peaceful sleep as the body leads the mind into slumber. And if you can practise a few minutes of meditation each day, you will be training your mind to know that it can have time off, so sleep should come more easily. It's a little like the trick of counting sheep in that sometimes it is very healthy to distract your mind so it can have a well-earned rest.

A good night's sleep

Did I dream of flittering about as a butterfly, or is the butterfly still dreaming that he is Chuang Tzu?
The philosopher Chuang Tzu

It is not important how many hours of sleep you have each night. What is important is that you wake up feeling refreshed and ready for the day ahead, however long you have been asleep. Here are some tips to help you:

- Managing your stress (see p. 206) is crucial in helping you to sleep well. Do things that you enjoy and that you know help you to unwind during the evening, like listening to music, reading or taking a bath.
- The Daily Breathing meditation (see p. 89) in the evening can help to relax both your mind and body as you begin to wind down a couple of hours before going to bed. When you are in bed you may also find it relaxing to visualise a beautiful place or scene, using all of your senses – say, you are walking along a beach listening to the sea, smelling the salt and feeling the sun on your face and the sand between your toes.
- Avoid drinking tea or coffee in the evening, which are stimulating; instead try relaxing drinks like herbal teas.
- You might fall asleep easily if you have drunk alcohol in the evening, but then wake up during the night and sleep fitfully thereafter. For a really good night's sleep it's best to avoid alcohol.
- Exercising in the evening can make it harder to relax and fall asleep, so try to exercise early in the evening or during the day.
- For a calm mind try to sleep mindfully – the bedroom should be a place for sleep, not for work.

- Get up early each morning at the same time, even if you are struggling to get to sleep at night. Over time this can help to create a sleep routine, and as you become more tired in the evenings you are more likely to be able to sleep. Likewise, don't be tempted to nap during the day.
- Keep active during the day, both mentally and physically if possible.
- In the moments before you drop off your consciousness straddles the two worlds of daily waking and sleeping. Take a moment to appreciate your life and you will trigger feelings of positivity that will go through your mind and body all through the night. You'll wake up refreshed and any seed of inspiration you plant is sure to have developed fresh green shoots ready for the day.

Get to know your restless signs

There is often a pattern to restlessness. And by getting to know and understand your mind through the meditations and being a bit more mindful or aware of your thoughts and emotions through your day-to-day life, you will be able to identify your own early signs of unrest. Checking in on yourself can prevent so much unnecessary discomfort and unhappiness.

The signs can be in your body as well as your

thoughts, your speech and behaviour. And rather than continue down the spiral of restlessness, so that you end up feeling exhausted, stressed, anxious, unhappy and even depressed, you will be able to notice what is happening early on and give yourself the nourishment you need. Because difficult things happen in life: you might find yourself getting lost in grief after losing a loved one, or that your responsibilities feel like they are piling up and weighing very heavily on you in uncertain times, or that work is just so very busy that you don't know if you'll be able to cope or feel you might collapse under the ever-growing list of targets and things you have to do.

Here are the signs to look out for:

- Is your mind becoming narrower? Are you having to decide what's important because you don't have enough time or energy to get things done? And what are you choosing? If you are sacrificing all the things that bring you joy and relaxation to spend all the hours of the day at work then how does that make your mind feel? Spacious and ready for anything or tight and stressed?
- Are you fully present with friends and family or does your mind constantly wander to other things? Do you worry about tomorrow's meeting while reading your daughter's bedtime

story, or come away from an evening with a friend feeling like you didn't manage to really talk deeply about anything?

- If you are a parent, do you feel guilty about constantly trying to juggle home and work life?
- Are you becoming more easily frustrated or angered by certain situations or people? Are you biting people's heads off, or somehow you can't seem to stop moaning?
- Are you letting exercise, which usually makes you feel really good, go by the wayside because you just don't seem to have the time for it any more?
- Are those familiar old thoughts about whether or not you are a 'good enough' person drifting back into your mind increasingly often?
- Are you eating well or are the takeaways and unhealthy foods creeping back into your diet because you're stressed and too tired to cook?
- Are you becoming more antisocial because you feel you need to put all your energy into work right now?
- Are you feeling more emotional than usual?
- Are you beginning to feel out of sorts, or that your life isn't well balanced in some way?

You may already be aware of how you tend to feel when life gets overwhelming or very stressful. You will be able to see or feel some of these signs early even with just a few minutes of the Daily Breathing exercise (see p. 89). The Self-reflection meditation (see p. 112) will fill in more of the detail of how your mind is becoming restless, while the Appreciation and Contemplating Change meditations (see pp. 102 and 107 respectively) are very good for helping to stop some of these feelings from growing deeper roots and becoming more fixed.

There may well be things that pull you off your path, and certain people or situations that always seem to push your buttons, but think about what is really making you restless in the long run – do your own feelings and reactions play a part? Is it time to take a different mental tack?

Find what is truly important in your life

When the mind becomes restless, tired or upset it is easy to lose perspective on life. You might sacrifice all the things you enjoy for the sake of one project at work, for example. The fear of failure or of not being thought of as 'good' becomes all-encompassing – more powerful even than the joy of putting your child to bed or seeing your best friend for a cup of coffee.

When you are in the eye of the storm, it's extremely hard to step back and ask yourself: is this is really what

I want? Is it the path to happiness? But if you practise when your mind is restful and you are feeling very good about life, you will gradually build up positive mental habits that can be of great help when you are under pressure.

Clearing the mind clutter

It is quite fascinating how our state of mind can usually be observed just by looking at our immediate surroundings. When you look at your desk or your tools as you are about to start work for the day what do you see? Is the path ahead nice and clear, or clogged up with lots of bits and pieces? Our possessions, or 'stuff', are such a clear reflection of our minds, whether we like to hoard and hold on to everything, for example, or whether we relish trips to the recycling centre and charity shop to make room for the new. But do your possessions help you to feel peaceful, happy or content?

A spring clean is an excellent practice for the restful mind, although sometimes it's not for the faint-hearted as you delve into cupboards and corners left untouched and full of clutter for years. Just as meditation is designed to create a sense of spaciousness in the mind, clearing our physical clutter can have a similarly positive effect. Just folding things neatly seems to create space we didn't realise we had. Clearing one's desk of all but one thing allows us to really focus and get that one thing done. We can breathe into our space and let things flow once again, rather than getting caught up in a mass of things we don't really need. After all, they've sat in the cupboard untouched for as long as we can remember.

When you next have a spring clean go right into the corners, even if you concentrate on just one room or even one drawer at a time. Some possessions can almost be like emotions: they rise up and cause us anxiety or negativity, and rather than taking a calm look at them, then allowing them to fade away, we push them back down. It's tempting to pull things out, then just hide them away again if you don't know what to do with them. But this time, why not let them go. Will you really miss them?

And once you have had a big clear out, then just like Daily Breathing or mindfulness practice, you might keep a gentle eye out for your things on a daily basis too, rather than just letting the clutter build up all over again. Just like our thoughts, if we don't pay attention for long periods of time, then it becomes an exhausting task to sort through everything.

Creating a sense of physical space has the instant effect of creating a feeling of space in the mind. Calm replaces panic and even time seems to stretch out once more. It's funny, but when you realise you can only focus on one thing right now, wear one coat or use one mug, you bring the art of simplicity back into your life, and letting go doesn't seem such a hard or bad thing after all. It releases you to get on with so much more, to really enjoy what you do have rather than continually going out to search for more.

Mindful cleaning

You might wonder if such a thing as cleaning can really be a mindfulness practice, but when you are relaxed and in the moment, the act of washing a plate can feel very calming and simply is what it is. It is often helpful to clean as you go, rather than leaving things to pile up or get very dirty. Think how relevant that is for the mind too. When you are cleaning, try not to spend the time thinking about all the other things you have to do – just clean.

Technology clutter

Technology has given us yet another opportunity to practise our hoarding tendencies. With the internet the answers to all our questions are at our fingertips, but then we end up holding so much information and so many questions in our minds when we should be enjoying dinner or a walk in the park with a friend, for example, that we are no longer really there.

As well as information overload, we seem to be burdened with communication overload too. Email inboxes are full to bursting – you might even be at that stage with yours of having to delete things on a daily basis just to let new messages in – and voicemails build up so that we can't even bring ourselves to listen to them all. Then there are all the blogs and interesting articles we want to read that we can file away for later at the touch of a button. Computers hold so much memory that we end up keeping everything 'just in case'. But our filtering systems have gone haywire, and just as you might wonder how you've ended up with so many plastic bags when you clear out your 'stuff', you feel overwhelmed by the inbox and the thought of tackling it now sends you into a mild panic. This can create a negative cycle: you worry that you don't have time to clear out the clutter, whether physical, technological or mental, but having it around is making matters worse, as you feel cramped and unfocused. It's as if your to-do list is surrounding you, with every little thing vying for your attention, saying, 'pick me, pick me'. Only you've lost the ability to work out what you need to pick next.

And while our social network may once have consisted of the three friends we went for a drink with at the weekend, now we are in touch with hundreds of virtual friends, colleagues or people we've never even met. But the funny thing is that despite being such a useful tool for communication, we often use technology as a way *not* to interact, to avoid potentially awkward conversations, like asking someone out on a date. We may send a Facebook message, which is safer for our emotions and our ego, but then we miss out on the emotional experience – and we also miss out on the lessons of such situations. If we never experience being turned down, then we never get to learn how to pick ourselves back up again.

Technology seems to be a source of restlessness for so many. It doesn't tell us what to do, but it does seem to provide so many choices. And when we don't know if we want WhatsApp, Facebook or LinkedIn, we have them all because we don't want to miss out.

So perhaps we can apply some aspects of the restful mind to this most modern of mental distractions. If you are struggling to stay on top of your technology clutter, think of the meditation on change: that nothing is fixed or permanent in our lives or the world around us, and so it is helpful not to become too attached to things. Just as the heads of companies seem to have very little clutter on their desks, their email inboxes are often fairly empty too. They tackle things as soon as they arrive, rather than holding on to them. Then they get on with something else, so that by the time others are just settling down at their desks with a coffee, the boss appears to be done for the day! So while it's true that they have big responsibilities, they manage not to be attached, which is the key to their success. And it is when they do become attached to specific outcomes that the mental anguish sets in for even the most successful people, as that is when fears creep in and their usual flexibility in tackling whatever ups and downs occur in the day becomes more rigid, vulnerable and prone to cracking.

If you can clear the tech clutter you will free up your mind to be much more present, rather than worrying about those messages you haven't replied to or those articles you haven't read. Give yourself the time to do this, even just a little at the end or beginning of the day to delete and therefore let go. The emails that you see right in front of you should be those you can address and deal with in the here and now, today. If they are from six months ago, how important are they really?

When Stress Gets the Better of Us

Disorders of the mind like chronic stress, anxiety and depression are becoming widespread in the modern world. Stress is now thought to be more of a risk factor when it comes to health than tobacco and can be a contributing factor in heart disease, muscle pain, chronic headaches, insomnia, weight loss and digestive disorders like IBS (irritable bowel syndrome).

Fight or flight

There is a part of the mind that is still very primitive, and in times of stress it literally takes over the body and prepares us to either fight or take flight. This fight-or-flight response was incredibly useful thousands of years ago when people were faced with bears and tigers. In such a stressful situation a shot of adrenalin would course through the body, and thinking things through would be replaced by an ability to react immediately, defend or attack.

In today's modern world you will still experience the fight-or-flight response, but often in mentally stressful situations, rather than physical. So if you become stressed – say, in a high-pressure meeting, or with the children screaming in the supermarket, going to the hospital or travelling to work – you will get the same shot of adrenalin your ancestors received facing a tiger, and like them, you might feel an intense need to fight (if not physically, then verbally) or flee the situation (slamming the door behind you).

These are the types of situation where a restful mind is put under great strain, even for the calmest of people. For many, anger or frustration will often rear up very quickly and be hard to control. You may find you are suddenly tearful or tense in your body. You literally see red, as rational thought goes out of the window.

Scientists tell us that fear and anxiety are not the same. Fear is the short-term response to an actual threat, while anxiety is the feeling that hangs around long after the threat has passed. Anxiety is also the feeling that comes when we worry about things that have yet to occur or may never occur. So while fear might be a very helpful response to get us to immediate safety in the present, anxiety seems to be a hangover from the past or a nervous anticipation or expectation of the future. We can use it to keep us on our toes and to stretch us beyond our comfort zone, but all too often it gets in the way of life.

Unfortunately, fear and anxiety can feel very similar – that's why anxiety is so uncomfortable, as it heightens all our senses while we might just be sitting at our desk or lying in bed at night. We feel it in the pit of our stomachs and our minds start whirring, its capacity for exaggeration seemingly unending.

But stress and its close bedfellow anxiety are not inherently bad. They come from our emotional, unconscious brain, and often a little stress is very motivating and gets us going, putting us in touch with our emotions, rather than always being ruled by our intellect. We find ourselves able to meet seemingly impossible deadlines and appreciate the energy boost in the times when we really need it. And within our anxiety we will often find aspects of ourselves that give us meaning and purpose, and the things we really want to do, if only we could be a little more sure of ourselves.

It is when these emotions take over and become overwhelming, however, that our minds become restless and uncomfortable, losing their sense of natural balance and feeling either wired or paralysed. The flow of our thoughts loses its rhythm, and we feel out of sorts, a bit 'all over the place' and unable to get things done. Then we begin to lose faith in ourselves, and we might become more demanding of others as we are less sure of our own self-nurturing capabilities.

Experts on stress suggest that you should look out for the following key factors:

- Feeling continuously overwhelmed
- Responding to your situation in a way that is constantly negative
- Overreacting to the stressor

When we feel very stressed we feel our minds are working against us. We overreact to situations that we could usually handle and it becomes difficult to see things clearly or make decisions. Feelings of fear and anxiety set in, creating an undercurrent of discomfort and affecting our thinking. We struggle to see the positive side of anything and so can't see how we are going to find a way out.

Breaking the cycle of the stressed mind

It is extremely hard to deal with stress well when it reaches the crisis point, when we are right in the thick of it. But if we can work on our minds when we are feeling good about ourselves, then this gives us great strength and resilience during more challenging times. Usually, when we are feeling good it's easy to ignore the mind as everything seems to be working very nicely. We feel the sense of spaciousness that is so crucial to the restful mind but will tend to take it for granted. It is only when things start to get difficult that we notice things aren't so happy in our mind, but without any preparation you can fall into the pattern of stress quite easily.

The Contemplation meditations that are included in the Mind Retreat (Part Two), especially the Appreciation and Contemplating Change meditations, are very helpful for training the mind so that when stressful situations arise you will be able to take them more in your stride. Even if only done for a few minutes each day they will allow you to notice what is going on in your life and, in the case of the Appreciation meditation, to particularly notice what is going right rather than what is going wrong. When you then contemplate change in all its aspects – accepting and even embracing that uncertainty is a part of life, and it is up to you how you react to it – you will find that your capacity to cope in the face of potentially stressful situations develops and grows with practice.

One of the best ways to calm the stressed mind is through the body. So just as stress affects your body in a negative way, you can use your body to reduce your stress to healthy levels. The Daily Breathing exercise (see p. 89) is especially helpful for lowering stress, and the more you practise, the more you will find that you can prevent stress from getting too high in the first place.

It is always better to train the mind before it reaches crisis level, but the Mind Retreat will work at any point. Since our minds are deeply influenced by our senses (what we hear, touch and so on), if our stress reaches a crisis level then physically retreating from such surroundings is recommended if possible. This is not running away from a situation. Rather, it is removing ourselves from the disturbing environment and then, in peaceful surroundings and with the tools of meditation, we will be able to see the situation clearly without being by blinded by emotions or physical discomfort. In a more relaxed environment we are much more likely to find a way to resolve things in the spaciousness of the natural state of mind and with compassion and understanding.

What are you being busy about?

Nature does not hurry, yet everything is accomplished.
Lao Tzu

How often do you or someone else say, 'I'm just rushing out of the door'? But where are we all rushing to? Why do we always feel the need to be so busy, so that we end up feeling like there is never enough time? It's great to have so much energy, but often the mind starts to feel very rushed too, as we pack so many things on to our to-do list that we end up flitting from one thing to another, rather than giving our full attention to any one of them.

A few minutes a day of meditation can be so beneficial for the rushed mind. As your focus and attention develop, your sense of time expands. As you contemplate life, you naturally begin to realise what is important versus the things that just cause you to run around feeling like you haven't really achieved anything well today. When you think about it, you do have time: all that time watching TV, surfing Facebook or asking Google so many questions. Be kind to yourself and say, 'I do have time'. Become the master to yourself. When you think you can't find the time in your own day, group meditation can be very helpful in getting you started with the mind exercises such as those in the Mind Retreat (see pp. 89–125).

We have so many opportunities in this modern world, but for many of us this has created a feeling of time becoming cramped and something which seems to always be against us. Then when we get to the end of the day, we assess everything we didn't manage to get done, rather than celebrating or exploring what we did achieve.

I think this very much goes back to the central theme of looking at where we are searching for happiness in our lives. Material success, a pat on the back and fitting in as many leisure activities and social engagements as we can are all supporting factors when it comes to happiness and contentment, but they are not the source. The reason we tend to pursue so many things in the day tends to boil down in some way or other to our perceived sense of happiness. We believe that taking on that extra work will make us feel useful and important, and therefore happy. Or if we can see all of our friends and family this month then somehow we will feel better about ourselves, and therefore happy. Or that working five extra hours today will mean that our boss sees how busy and helpful we are and will think good things, which will in turn make us feel secure, and therefore happy.

The thing is that while we are filling up time with these pursuits we are still looking for happiness outside of ourselves. If, on the other hand, we look within ourselves for happiness, then we may begin to manage time based on what is truly important; we will pursue fewer things, and will focus and concentrate on what we are doing, who we are talking to, right now.

Consumed by overthinking and worries

If there is something you can do to fix it then fix it; if there is nothing you can do then don't worry there is no point.

Shanti deva, Indian master

Many of us appear to go about our daily business quite well – we have friends and/or family who love us, a good job, a good life. But underneath it all there is often an undercurrent of anxiety or worry that pervades everything: will I still have my job by the end of this recession? What if I mess something up really badly? Did I offend so and so by not inviting her to my birthday party? What if the car fails its MOT? – I need it to drive to work and we can't afford a new one . . .

Worries are like habits of the mind too, in that you can easily fall into a pattern of feeling anxious about things; even if you don't expect the worst to always happen, you may worry about the possibility of it at length. Worrying is overthinking, and especially about the uncertainties of the future and how you are perceived by others. You may worry about a phone call – concerned that it could be difficult when, in fact, the other person just wants to have a chat or ask you something simple. You might be understandably worried about money, but rather than think things through and rest in the knowledge you can't control everything and that you are as prepared as you can be, you continue to fret endlessly about all the things that are out of your control, even though you know deep down it is a waste of your mental energy.

Some people get into the habit of thinking the worst. Perhaps quite a few bad things have already happened to them, so expecting the worst is a way of bypassing the disappointment of when hopes and dreams aren't realised: if you think the worst, you can't be disappointed. But the mind doesn't work well that way, because pessimism rarely leads to a real sense of happiness. You might be surprised by something good happening for a moment, but the undercurrent of pessimism is still there, waiting for the next blow. The pessimistic mind has strong walls all around it, blocking our vision and keeping us closed off from the potential of life. In the search for comfort in the knowledge that things can't be worse than we imagine, we end up feeling disappointed in our lack of courage and wish we could broaden our horizons and take a leap once in a while.

And just as many people are fearful of what the future may hold, others are trapped in the past. They may worry constantly about things they have said or done; whether their words or actions upset others or will cause their own suffering in some way. Or perhaps they feel extremely nostalgic for the past, seeing things through rose-tinted glasses, so that when they compare the present to the past they feel somewhat disappointed.

Although this is a book dedicated to the mind, this is a good place to say that many people can suffer from thinking too much. They examine a conversation had earlier in the day, week or even year and analyse it over and over again. The problem is that they usually only analyse from their own point of view and are often surprised and confused by how others see exactly the same situation.

Instead of making things more painful by over-thinking and imagination going on overtime, we should relax and then check what we can actually do about it. Reflect on why we are causing distress to ourselves. What is the benefit of such a state of mind?

Helping your mind to slow down

Tension is who you think you should be.
Relaxation is who you are.
Chinese Proverb

We are all so distracted in today's world, rushing, both physically as we go from one appointment to the next, and in our minds, which are flitting from one task or thought to the next. So how can we help the mind to slow down?

- If you tend to occasionally or even regularly feel consumed by worries, the Mind Retreat meditations (see Part Two) are very helpful for gradually regaining a sense of perspective and space. Worries are usually negative thoughts that go round and round about either small or big things. They often imagine the worst when we really don't know what the outcome of a situation will be. Give yourself time in the day to practise breathing in positive, calm and confident white light while breathing out your worries as black smoke (see p. 92–93). As you do the Appreciation and Contemplating Change meditations (see pp. 102 and 107 respectively) you will gently encourage your mind to see what you cherish and want to nurture in your life.

- Doing less. It can be hard to pause long enough to think about what you are doing, but in the long run this will give you more time and space to focus on and enjoy the things and people in your life that matter. Contemplate what is really important in your life today; decide on your priorities and practise saying 'No'.

- You don't have to try and rid your mind of all distractions; rather, as they drift into your mind, let them drift off too, and don't hold on to them so tightly. It might be that something you think of as just an annoyance or a distraction could actually be something much more fulfilling if you bring yourself fully into its presence in the moment. So instead of fighting against distraction, become an observer of it, not a slave.

- Letting go of fussiness or perfection will help to slow down your restless mind. Why keep trying to be something that is impossible? Why try to reach somewhere that leaves you with nowhere else to go?
- Bring a little mindfulness into the simple things in your day and you will find you can bring yourself back into the present, rather than always rushing around in your thoughts to things that have already been or are yet to come. Sit quietly with a cup of tea. Spend five minutes just walking and observing nature or the city around you. Savour the preparation and eating of your daily meals – get caught up in chopping, even the washing up! There can be beauty in every task and every moment if we let ourselves feel it.
- Try to do one thing at a time, rather than moving constantly between one task and another while thinking about three others.

The mindful reaction

Stress is a response that sets off a physical and emotional reaction in our body almost in an instant (see p. 203).

So how can we stop it happening if we only have an instant? We won't always be able to stop the stress response, and sometimes there is a very good reason for that because we need to be on high alert in a particular situation or need to engage all of our survival instincts. But for those everyday situations, like a traffic jam or the bus that never comes, we can work on learning how to react in a more relaxed way. And, as with everything, it's something that becomes increasingly easy through practice.

The traffic jam

Peace comes from within. Do not seek it without.
Buddha

Being stuck in a traffic jam or a long queue is an everyday challenge to the restful mind that so many people face. What happens to your mind as you sit or stand with a feeling that you have nowhere to go? Perhaps you started the day on the wrong side of bed and everything has gone against you since then. And as you try to wait patiently, someone rushes out of nowhere to push in ahead. Maybe you try an alternative route, change queue and end up worse off than if you had stuck to your first option. You can't believe how much time you are wasting just waiting to get to where you need to go. And then you start to panic that you might be late and you've got that important meeting: your shoulders tense up, your breath gets shallow. You feel frustrated in both your body and your mind. And while all this is happening, there is the nagging reality that you can't do anything about it. And that frustrates you even more.

Now look at that reality again: 'you can't do anything about it'. It's true to the extent that you can't control the external conditions that are causing you to be stuck in a jam, queue jumped by other people or late for that meeting. But what you can have some control over is how you react to this frustrating situation. Do the other drivers or passengers care that you are going to be late? Will your rage help you feel any better, either in the moment or when you reach your destination? Does it have to ruin your whole day? Is the world really out to get you today? These are the things you do have control over; it's not to say that you won't feel frustration rise up when inching along the motorway or stuck in a tunnel. But, with practice, you can realise that you don't have to hold on to the frustration or feed it. You can give yourself a little space through breathing, and even by not driving quite so bumper-to-bumper with the car in front. And you can accept that sometimes things just don't go according to plan. And you should also think about how understanding people usually are when it comes to you letting them know you're stuck in traffic or on a train. It's happened to us all. So try to be as understanding with yourself: you can't make the traffic disappear, you'll get to where you're going as soon as you possibly can, and even if you're late for that meeting or plane

– or even miss them altogether – life really does have a way of moving on, and most of the time working things out, especially if we let it.

Learn to use the body to calm the mind in moments of stress. You can do this by coming back to the breath; it is the essence of all life when you think about it and is the best way to bring yourself back into the present. By focusing on the breath you don't just take the heat out of the moment, you also get to sit with your emotions. You don't have to feel bad about them, but rather can see them for what they are. It's human to get frustrated and wish things to be another way sometimes, but when you give these emotions a bit of space, you can often see that although, yes, in this moment, you really are fed up, you cannot make the bus appear out of thin air or turn your boss into the most lovely person on earth. As your body begins to calm down through breathing more evenly, often your mind calms too; and so even though the stress or emotion might still be present, it is no longer consuming you.

The act of going for a walk often has the same effect; just a few minutes around the block can bring the mind back into more of a sense of balance. These restful mind tools of breathing and contemplation might not solve all of our problems all of the time. Nothing in life can do that. But they can affect how we react to and then address our challenges. Do we let them bring us down or can we acknowledge that we are trying our best and so give ourselves a break?

When you *think* you can't see a way out

There are times in life when you not only face challenges or everyday ups and downs, but a crisis or catastrophe – when it feels as though a bomb has exploded in your head or your heart. It might seem that the mind can be anything but restful during such times, but it can at least be of some help with how you cope and how you come out of a crisis on the other side.

First off, if you think you can't see a way out of a situation, then you need to ask for help in whatever form is comfortable or useful to you individually. This might be professional help, or it might be seeking out those friends and loved ones who you know you can turn to for wisdom and compassion, who seem to just have a way about them that can help your mind see things a little more clearly. These aren't the people who simply always say what you want to hear, but equally they don't push their own agendas on to you. They have a way of listening, seeing things from your point of view and also gently coming up with positive ways forward all at the same time. Or they may be people who make you feel more peaceful within yourself so that you are able to navigate troubled waters with a little more calm. Think about who these people might be in your life. It is good to contemplate these relationships as they help us to tap into the wise friend within ourselves too, and to show compassion to our own friends when in times of need.

If you practise the meditations in the Mind Retreat (Part Two), then you will find that if something terrible does happen in your life, you might be better equipped in your mind to cope with it. The meditations are not designed to take away your sadness or upset, and you still feel emotions very deeply, but you will gradually develop a perspective on life that can help you to see the good, however small, in a situation. You can realise that while letting go of hurt doesn't mean you didn't really feel it, it's just that to continue holding on brings unnecessary suffering. And you realise that although when going through difficult situations they feel like they will never end, at some point they *will* feel like a dream.

The most difficult time to see a way out is in the heat of a crisis. Losing your job, your house or your partner may cause you to experience panic, anger, any number of extreme emotions that in their turn cloud the mind even further, so that you are really struggling to see any way forward. You may think: it's all very well for you monks, sitting on your mountains, but what about when the real world turns against you and you feel like you are about to lose everything?

I hope that as you read this book and begin to understand how you can transform your own mind, you may find it helpful – even in very difficult situations. Your awareness is already beginning to grow as you observe how your mind and emotions flow during the day, and perhaps you are starting to feel less attached to things that don't go so well, worrying a little less about what might happen in the future and making the most of the present day. Perhaps you are being less quick to criticise or to feel frustrated, as you are developing your appreciation and also realising that we are all different and yet the same, and what a good thing that might be in our lives.

If we are less grasping in our attachment to things like a job or a house, then rather than seeing only suffering in losing them, we might see the glimmer of possibility. We might understand that houses, jobs and people do all come and go in life, and we can't always control when. So while we might feel that it's far too soon, or that it isn't fair, or wonder why bad things happen to good people, we might also look for the potential lesson or even opportunity and then focus our energy on nurturing that little piece of good so that it expands and helps to balance out life once again. In some way, an end is always a beginning.

The Restful Mind at Work

Restlessness and anxiety in the mind are often triggered in the work environment. The pressure to succeed, to get everything right and to avoid blame are often extremely prevalent. And the constraints of time and how to get everything done worry a great many people. Work relationships can cause anxieties too, especially as there are often power issues at play. You might feel that another person is constantly on your case, or that your success in life to some degree depends on their decisions about you. And then there are the daily anxieties about whether a meeting or telephone call will go well or not, how people will react to your presentation, whether you complete your work on time or miss that crucial deadline.

Work can be a source of great joy in life; you can feel like you are really contributing, caring or creating through your own individual skills and passions. But it is also where the ego can feel extremely vulnerable. The culture in which you work is important to be aware of. Unfortunately, there are workplaces where blame is a part of the atmosphere, creating an underlying fear of getting anything wrong. This can play havoc with the mind as you worry about all the what-ifs constantly. You might continue to go about your daily tasks, but spend an unhealthy amount of time in the evenings or at the weekends worrying about work, your status there and what the management may or may not be thinking of you.

In many work environments there is a strong sense of competition, encouraged to promote getting the best out of all the employees. This can often seem to work very well, on a superficial level at least. People work very hard to be the number-one salesperson, the one who gets the next available promotion or the highest bonus. And yet this underlying current of competition can also have a negative effect on the mind at work. Instead of celebrating in the efforts and successes of colleagues, you might focus instead on comparing your own achievements with theirs. This constant pressure can build up, so that stress levels never get a chance to come back to a healthy equilibrium, and even your health might be affected, from struggling to sleep right through to the health of your heart.

It is very understandable that we all want to do well in our work, receive positive feedback and progress along our career paths. It also makes sense that we might not choose for all of our work colleagues to be our friends or loved ones. Sometimes we are thrown together with people who don't naturally bring out the best in us, who we wouldn't consider our wisdom gurus; but if we think about it, work can be one of the best teachers for us in our practice to become more appreciative, patient and compassionate in life.

It is interesting that in Bhutan, where happiness is a primary goal of the country as a whole, the culture is not to work long hours, and so cultivate the balance between work and home. People have plenty of time to relax and be with their family or friends. Salaries may not be as high as in other countries, but the people seem very happy to be able to pay their rent and have enough, rather than always competing for more. This is just the cultural experience in one small country, but perhaps as individuals we may learn a little from this and see the value in a balanced life, rather than sacrificing one part of it for another.

The power of intention

When we believe that things outside of us determine our happiness we tend to focus on outcomes more than intention as our driving force: a new job with a bigger salary, a girlfriend, a slimmer body, a pat on the back at work. And yes, we can reach those goals, but often the happiness that comes with reaching them is only temporary. We meet the girl of our dreams and we are so happy, and things are just perfect. But then, one day, they are not quite as we want them to be, and we're not so happy then. Or we get a slimmer body in time for a holiday, but hate all the foods we had to eat to get to that point, so we go back to the way we used to eat and just end up feeling guilty for putting the weight back on. Or, even worse, we never reach the goal and feel upset and disappointed in ourselves and in life.

You might think that without goals, especially career goals, you will never reach beyond your comfort zone to make life better, to provide more for your family, to do great work for others. But what I would ask you to do is to look at the *intentions* behind your goals and start from there when you go about your day. If you start the day with good intention, then you glance inwards, before you look outwards, and, in the process, you become more mindful of what you are going to do today. In this way you become more involved in your tasks, rather than thinking of them as just something you have to do in order to get that raise or promotion, or to be 'more successful' than that colleague who always seems to do so well. Just thinking about the task itself brings you back into the present.

Take the examples I used of finding a job with a bigger salary, a girlfriend, a slimmer body and a pat on the back at work. We can turn all of them around to be intention-driven, rather than outcome-focused. So instead of scouring the job sites just for bigger salaries, think about the work you want to do and how you might spend time really focusing on making your resumé as interesting as possible, so that it reflects how you would like to progress in your career. Or instead of imagining a girlfriend, think about the person you would like to be in a relationship with and go out for an evening with your friends in that frame of mind. And instead of just seeing yourself slimmer, think about how you want to change what you eat or how you might exercise for the better. As for the desire for the pat on the back at work – that becomes an intention to simply do great work today. If someone likes it, then great, if we don't get praised, it doesn't matter – it's the work that counts.

If you can make this change in your daily life, then your mind will thank you. Because when you are outcome-driven you are trying to control that which is impossible to control. Again, you are looking to fix what is on the outside, rather than on exactly where you can make a difference – and that is your intention. Everything else will flow from there.

Joyful effort

In every walk of life there is the opportunity to help people from your heart with your skills and talents, through hard but enjoyable work. Don't you deserve a job you love?

The feeling that we are contributing and doing good work has a positive effect on all aspects of our lives. In a way, then, we need to listen a bit more to our inner wisdom when it comes to regaining a sense of joyful work. Our egos may want trophies and recognition, but our true natures want to do really good work, and for us to be able to enjoy ourselves while we're at it. We want to get lost in the flow, to smile with our colleagues and give our skills and talents to the world in whatever way we can.

Often it isn't the work itself that makes us feel restless or stressed, but all the things that build up around it. You often have to deal with different types of people, which can make you feel frustrated or misunderstood. You have to wait for others to make decisions, sit in meetings which you think are a waste of time or where you feel irrelevant. Technology doesn't help matters, as messages mount up and threads of email conversations become ever more complicated and difficult to keep track of. Many people find that they are constantly interrupted, and so can't seem to get any tasks done. They blame the work environment for their restlessness and inability to focus, for not making that phone call or for spending a whole day procrastinating over something on their to-do list, and so getting very little done except a whole lot of worrying.

It can be helpful, therefore, to remind ourselves to turn the spotlight inwards, rather than falling into the habit of looking outside ourselves to check how our work life is going and might be improved or made more joyful. A woman from Peru who attended one of our retreats described how she had used some of the restful mind exercises in her work. She had a very interesting and fulfilling job as a museum designer, working in the Machu Picchu Museum in the mountain city of Cusco. She had to travel all around the country to understand where certain artifacts came from and their cultural context. As a mountain person, what she found most challenging was visiting river or forest cultures, often only reachable by a small boat and accompanied by just a photographer and a guide. She would feel quite fearful and the river people she met would sometimes be defensive and have very different ways and ideas. So she decided to think about how really we are all the same: 'They were just like me, with the same wish for happiness, and not to suffer.' This simple thought lessened her worries about difference and created a bridge over which she could connect with them, and so improve her work. Just changing her own attitude a little also had the effect of softening the people she met.

Commitment is freeing

We have talked quite a bit about how grasping on too tightly to attachments – whether material possessions or relationships, for example – can be a source of restlessness, causing us to spend too much time worrying about the things we might lose, rather than enjoying what we have today.

However, to free your mind from restlessness is not to give up on your commitments. When you commit to something with your heart and mind, you really free yourself to get on with it. You are the boss; you have made the commitment. It's always up to you. Even when you think there are no external choices in this life, there is a choice you can make within your mind. Commitments are such choices.

When you commit you become dedicated and diligent about whatever it is you are doing. This helps greatly with concentration and focus in the moment. It is when you listen to your inner nature and remember or discover for the first time what is truly important in your life that you are able to commit and free yourself from all the ifs, buts and maybes that come when you are not ready or are afraid of what might or might not happen. You are no longer so attached to very specific outcomes, but rather make a commitment from within, and then know that you must do your best. You cannot control other people or the world around you, but you can commit to playing your own part – in this way commitment can be very uplifting.

You could even be happy with your boss

For many people, this might be the ultimate happiness! We may spend a great deal of our life at work and so to have good relationships with colleagues can bring much relief to a restless mind. This is especially the case with a manager or boss, where the imbalance of power can make us worried and feel vulnerable. We never feel quite secure with them. And when we judge and criticise how *they* do things we further upset the calm balance of our minds, frustrated that they have more responsibility and more money, when we could do the job better.

Contemplating the themes of attachment, projection and yes, even appreciation, when it comes to our boss can go a long way towards being more relaxed and happy at work. We often place far too much attachment on their words of praise or blame, judging our performance by a barometer that we forget also has a great deal to do with how they are feeling in their own mind that day, how they are feeling about *their* boss and whether they are feeling the pressures of expectation or happily going with the flow. One day we feel buoyed up by a big pat on the back and the next it all comes crashing down as the boss jumps on a mistake we have made. We feel unsure as to where we stand because we have forgotten to be self-reliant and confident that we will come in each day and do our best.

It is a good idea to remember that we are all just human beings, even at work! We are all special, and yet not very special at the same time. It is easy to get caught up in the power struggles that so often seem to be present within the work environment; if this is something that can make you feel anxious or agitated, drawn in to competing and comparing or that seems to knock your confidence on a weekly basis, then have the courage and the daring to be different. Encourage yourself to stand back from the battle of the egos and stay true to your inner nature.

Procrastination

Why are we sometimes so easily distracted from the work at hand? We can spend a whole day thinking about making a phone call without actually making it. We'll convince ourselves that no one wants to be called first thing in the morning, so wait and busy ourselves with another task even though our mind is still half on the call we need to make. Then a few hours pass and we think, no one wants to be called at lunchtime, so wait and find something else to do, without really focusing on it or doing it properly. And then we let the afternoon drift by and think it must be too late to call – we'll do it first thing in the morning.

Deadlines seem to bring out the worst and then suddenly the best in us. We have a month to get a report done, so we spend three weeks thinking about the fact that we really should make a start and then three days at the end of the month working like mad to get it finished on time. We wonder why we left it so late, wasting all that time thinking and not actually doing anything. We wonder what we could achieve if we could just get on with things.

- The Appreciation meditation (see p. 102) is very good for helping us to get on with our day in a more energetic, active way. Appreciating things in life is very motivating. We might not say in the morning, 'I am so lucky to have this particular task', but we do nourish an appreciation of the positive aspects of our work, rather than focusing on the things we might be tempted to moan or gripe about. You can also adapt this type of meditation for the beginning of the work day. When we procrastinate little seeds of negativity develop in our mind, and then our imagination gets in on the act, making things worse. So we put off making that phone call because we start imagining that it won't go very well or we worry that our report might not be of a high enough standard. But we can use our minds to turn these thoughts around; we might say to ourselves: I'm going to smile as I imagine the person on the other end of the phone, just be really nice and take it from there. Or that we are going to get really stuck in to that report today and find one brilliant thing that everyone can take from it.

- Doing something differently can break you out of the habit of procrastination, just as it can help with any type of habit. Try sitting somewhere different with no distractions like your in-tray or your phone. Just take one thing to do and make a start, with no pressure on yourself to finish there and then.

- Focus on doing one thing well, rather than thinking about five different tasks at once and never getting started on any of them. Our minds often try to tackle everything at once, while in reality we can only do one thing at a time. Even if we say we are multi-tasking, in the moment we are doing just one thing, even if we are moving between different plates to keep them all spinning. And to be honest, when spinning plates we are mostly just running between them, wasting time and mental energy switching from one task to another and back again.

- However long your to-do list is today, pick one thing at the beginning of the day and focus on getting it done. And putting everything else aside, give that one task your full attention. Even if it's one incredibly important phone call you have been putting off and might only take a few minutes, do it today and your restless mind will breathe again. Let go of the idea that you can get everything done today and you will be surprised at just how much you can achieve once your mind has the space in which to work.

Meetings

Meetings can be very creative and motivating, but they can also be quite stressful, boring or feel like a waste of time. Maintaining a restful, focused mind throughout can be a challenge. It is easy to let the mind wander, to not really be present. But although we might not always have a great deal to say in a meeting, it can be a very good place to practise our listening and observational skills. We can decide to be generous with our time and really pay attention to our colleagues, supporting them in their ideas if we like them or simply taking note about how a project is going. If we let our mind just wander all over the place, then we will often miss out on what is happening right now, and we will not really achieve anything in our minds either.

There is something to be gained from every moment in life. We hate irrelevance because we think it's a waste of precious time, but things that are seemingly irrelevant can be great teachers. We might listen to how a colleague in another department does something and realise how applicable their methods might be to our own tasks. If we listen intently, we might see a side of a colleague we never knew was there. And sometimes in a meeting we can just be and see what happens.

What is boredom? How can we avoid it?

When the joy goes out of our effort we can easily become bored. Rather than being present with the task at hand we are distracted, unfocused and looking for the next shiny new thing. I think boredom comes because we are unable to relax in the natural state of mind and we need constant entertainment or distraction. The moment that we feel a slight sense of boredom approaching, our reaction will often be to feel more agitated, both in mind and body. It is related to our perception that our joys and pains come from external sources which always keep us looking for something without us knowing exactly what that something is.

As well as practising with the Daily Breathing exercise (see p. 89), try looking into the nature of the bored mind. What is it? Where does it come from? I was not bored yesterday, why am I bored today? Have things changed or has my perception changed?

Calming your nerves

Whether it's a job interview, making a phone call or giving a presentation, nerves can set our minds on edge and make us feel very uncomfortable. Many of us don't mind this feeling once in a while, if we are lucky enough to be able to cope with our nerves, but if you are someone who feels paralysed by nerves or would like to take some of the heat out of them, then a couple of the key mind tools are particularly good to practise.

Bringing your focus back to your breath will relax your body and distract your mind from all your nervous thoughts. Come back into the present moment and engage in your immediate surroundings, rather than getting caught up in anxious 'what-if' thoughts.

For example, if you are in a job interview, stop analysing your own answers, worrying about what you just said or what the interviewer might ask next. Come back into the moment and you will realise you are really just talking to another person. Pause, breathe gently and also listen. By allowing the interview to become a two-way street we can connect with the person and even enjoy the experience. After all, you may well have lots in common and might have a really interesting conversation. Speak from your heart and, whether you get the job or not, you can't go wrong as you will be true to yourself and come across that way too, rather than trying to play some kind of role or tick all the right boxes.

Finding a quiet space at work

The techniques of meditation can be used in even the busiest of environments like a crowded shop or train, but if we can remove ourselves for a few moments to a quiet, peaceful place then the effects are even stronger. Taking ourselves away from an environment of tension makes it easier to release the tension in our own minds. When we step back physically we may also step back mentally, take a pause to reflect and observe how we're feeling; just by taking that moment to observe and become aware may help us be less consumed by thoughts or emotions that have been triggered.

If, however, you can never be alone at work to collect your thoughts, then still engage in the Daily Breathing exercise (see p. 89) to help to slow things down for a couple of minutes and bring yourself back into your body, especially if you feel as though negative emotions or words are bubbling very close to the surface.

I have met many people during my travels who work in places where there are lots of people involved; whether in a company, a charity like our Live to Love organisation, in hospitals, government departments, every type of organisation. Often these people will tell me that there are two key messages that help them feel better on a daily basis however stressful their job. The first is that it really helps to understand that *we can't control every outcome*. There are too many people and various other conditions involved that we can't hope to feel ok if we did try to affect the outcome of all decisions in the company. The second message is then related to the first in that it helps to remind ourselves not to be results orientated but to be motivation orientated. It is good to always focus on your intention and know at the end of the day you have tried your best, whatever the outcome. In this way, we can take care of our restful mind and put our energies into our actual work, rather than our worries about it.

The restful decision

The choices that you make are all stepping stones on your path. Often, you might agonise over making the right or wrong decision, but there really is no right or wrong, and every step you take becomes a part of your experience and learning. Nevertheless, you want to try to make choices that are well considered, where you listen to both your rational mind and your heart.

His Holiness Gyalwang Drukpa has a brilliant philosophy – to try to be 'spontaneous and well prepared'. It is a wonderful piece of advice for life, and especially when making decisions, because if we are both spontaneous and well prepared, then we will use these two precious parts of our mind in harmony – our emotions as well as our intellect. So we do our research, we look at our decision from all angles, but we also allow ourselves to *feel* our decision, to sometimes just go for it and take a leap.

Use all of your senses to stimulate your thoughts and emotions. You might make a pot of your very favourite tea to put yourself in a relaxed, happy state of mind. Ideally, it is better to be calm before taking decisions. Consider your choices from different sides and angles, don't be fixed in your ideas and try not to look into the future to see the outcomes. Consult the people in your life who connect well with your inner nature and often help with finding your direction. These are the people who will listen openly and encourage you in your own decision, rather than pushing you too heavily in one direction or another.

Think again of being intention-driven and then open to whatever the outcome may be. Often some of the best experiences in life come from the most unexpected situations. Things don't always go according to plan and that's why life is so rich and fascinating.

> It is thought that going to a high place is very helpful for making decisions, and for meditation generally if you are able. This is because you have a better view of the world, you can see more of what is in front of you, both physically and perhaps mentally too (see p. 88).

A Mind Full of Love

The thought manifests as the word. The word manifests as the deed. The deed develops into the habit. And the habit hardens into character. So watch the thought and its ways with care. And let it spring from love.
Buddha

The main purpose of the restful mind is that we have more room for and capacity to love; to let ourselves care very deeply and then live life accordingly. If we can let go of being so strongly attached to how we think things and people should be, then we can be even more generous in our love – a love that doesn't require thank-you notes from those we love, but for which we ourselves are thankful every day. This type of love brings balance into our lives; it is a love full of peace. It is generous to others through the way in which we think, speak and act. It's the kind of love that is a really good habit to have. Buddhists talk about the love of a mother for her only child as the best example of love without attachment. There are no conditions. Even if we don't agree with everything they do, even if sometimes they seem to not even want our love, it is just there.

This kind of love – that we can adapt to all our relationships – is very nourishing to the general atmosphere, whether within the family, at work or even as we stand in line for a cup of coffee. In time, you may even begin to notice a change in those around you as a result of your changing from within.

One of the biggest obstacles to love is frustration. We load expectations on to the people we love and also on ourselves and how we should be in our relationships – as a partner, a father, a mother, son, daughter, sister, brother. We grasp on too tightly to the way we want things to be, trying to arrange for the world around us, including our relationships, to be a certain way. We want to be respected, to be constantly admired. But this sets us up for lots of potential restlessness when, inevitably, people don't always quite act or say things the way we would like.

Family love

A family is a place where minds come in contact with one another. If these minds love one another, the home

> *will be as beautiful as a flower garden. But if these minds get out of harmony with one another, it is like a storm that plays havoc with the garden.*
>
> Buddha

It is natural to want the best for our loved ones, to be proud of their achievements and be protective. But when we are attached to our expectations we can often become very fixed and rigid in what we think is best, and so are often frustrated or disappointed when other people don't turn out according to our plans. Wanting to be a guide, protector and mentor for the people we love is why we survive and grow as humans. The key, perhaps, is to try and always do this from the depths of your compassionate heart, so from your inner nature, rather than your ego. Allow and encourage your family to be their own people, listen when they talk to you, don't be so quick to judge or criticise and offer happiness wherever and whenever you can.

I am not a parent, but combining what I have learned from my spiritual teachers with what I observe, I would like to say only that the most important thing is that we bring up our children with love, understanding and wisdom, and we try our best to create favourable conditions for them in life. At the same time, it is important to realise that we cannot really control their destiny. We have to remember that while we might feel indispensable to the world in general and to our children in particular, in reality, life will go on for the world in our absence, as well as for our children, just as it does for us in the absence of our own parents and of so many great beings of the past. There is a Tibetan saying that all children come with their own store of joys and sadness, and while parents can help, only they themselves really transform their lives. Therefore, as parents we should do our best with love and wisdom, and have satisfaction that we did so; but, at the same time, we have to realise that to control the destiny of others is impossible.

When responsibilities get you down

There are times when we carry our responsibilities in life as burdens, weighing our minds down. This is when we have lost our sense of appreciation for how precious life is, as well as that feeling of being so very lucky.

It is true that sometimes life is very challenging and that you do things you are not so happy about for the sake of others, like dragging yourself into work each day because you have to provide for your family, for example. And in these times, the Appreciation and Contemplating Change meditations (see pp. 102 and 107 respectively) can help to make you present with what truly matters in life, giving you the motivation and momentum to strive to nourish those things, rather than allowing less desirable things in life to take over and affect everything else.

You can't always control what job you have or what house you live in, or even whether your family will appreciate what you do for them every day, but you can control what you want to focus on: you can decide to provide them with unconditional love because these are the people with whom you share your happiest moments. You don't have to carry your responsibilities as a pressure or heavy burden that makes your heart feel like it is sinking, like your energy is stuck, instead of flowing free. It is up to you – you really don't have to depend on others to set you free.

Love and desire

If we can be aware of the nature of our attachment when it comes to desire and loving relationships, then we can help ourselves through those times when our minds are struggling or we are creating obstacles for ourselves.

Think of the 'mind games' that people end up playing in relationships when there has been some kind of breakdown of trust or mutual respect, compassion and kindness. Whether there was a specific trigger or communication has been eroded gradually over time, for some reason you feel caught up in negative thoughts that, in turn, feed how you act and speak with your partner. You might have begun to worry they don't love you as much any more, and so you say anything or do anything you can think of to get their attention. You tell them about the other people who give you attention or you start looking at other people in the room. You might begin to fixate on small habits of theirs that never used to bother you, but suddenly make you feel like screaming.

At the beginning of a relationship it is easy to be

appreciative without even thinking about it; you can't believe this amazing person chose you, and you can't believe how lucky you are to have found love. But it is just as easy to start taking relationships for granted, forgetting how grateful we once were to have found this person.

As you practise the Appreciation meditation (see p. 102) for a few minutes each day, you might rediscover your deep gratitude for the love of your partner and the love you give to them, especially when you also contemplate the nature of how things change (see p. 107), and that change isn't such a bad thing, but opens up new opportunities and possibilities, both for you as an individual and for your relationships.

We each bring our own experiences and thoughts to our relationships every day; our relationships navigate the waves, the ups and downs of two people's lives. No wonder they feel the strain occasionally. The things that tend to disrupt our happiness when it comes to relationships often relate back to our outer egos and whether we tend to seek happiness outside of ourselves or within. Just as we have patterns and habits in the way we think that have built up through our lifetimes, we often have set beliefs in the way we think about relationships, and the way we think we are in relationships. We may, for example, have a belief that eventually everyone leaves us, so that even though a relationship is going very well, we might begin to sabotage it as our negative thoughts begin to grasp at the darker clouds that naturally come overhead, and we stop noticing all the clear skies in between. We might have been hurt in the past, and so find it difficult to be trusting of our partner, so we begin to question their movements or become more clinging.

We might also bring strong beliefs to our relationships about how others should be, and so get frustrated when our partner displays behaviour we 'don't like'. This is why it can be so helpful to remind ourselves through contemplation meditations (see pp. 96–121) that we are all different and yet all the same too. We all have ways of seeing and being that have built up through our own experiences of life, but at the heart of it all we all want to be happy, to be loved and to love. Perhaps we might find it easier then, to let go of some of our fussiness about how people should be, especially the person closest to us; we might appreciate each day together even more and spend less time looking to the future and worrying about things that might go wrong. Relationships do, of course, go wrong, and while you must not ignore your deep instincts about how things are or stay when things are bad, you shouldn't sabotage yourself when things are good.

*To wake at dawn with a winged heart and give thanks
for another day of loving;
To rest at the noon hour and meditate love's ecstasy;
To return home at eventide with gratitude;
And then to sleep with a prayer for the beloved in your
heart and a song of praise upon your lips.*
Kahlil Gibran, *The Prophet*

Keeping calm with the people who drive us mad

Fights would not last if only one side was wrong.
François de La Rochefoucauld

As we work on our minds and begin to feel more calm and restful, we naturally develop our compassion and consideration for others. This is the emotional intelligence that allows us to step outside of our own minds and into someone else's shoes, even when they are pressing all our buttons. We still might disagree with them wholeheartedly, but we have done our best to see things from their perspective, and also to understand that there is no 'right' or 'wrong' view. Even if they appear to want to drive us mad, we can move on and use the experience as a lesson that the right view does not exist.

With the difficult people in your life, externally try to always gently explain your point of view while trying to see theirs, and internally be extra kind. We will never change anybody's mind or ways through forceful words or acts. And sometimes we have to realise when there is nothing we can do to make a person like us, but we can still be kind in our thoughts, words and actions towards them because the only person suffering from our frustration and disappointment, our attachment to somehow winning them over, is us. Different people look at the world in different ways. And while we will always try to bridge those different views, there are some people in our life who will just never travel to meet us halfway.

Strategies for dealing with difficult people

- Don't get into a game of ping-pong with difficult people, where each of you seems to bring out the worst in each other; one hurt followed by another. Don't be afraid to keep your distance, and at the same time ask yourself: when I get angry with them, does it make me happy? Why am I making myself suffer?

- It is helpful to be aware that the faults we see in others are often those we see in ourselves, so if you find yourself being very critical of another person, investigate this and check in on yourself, through the contemplation meditations (see pp. 96–120).

- When you are feeling in a calm and positive state of mind, look at a picture of the person who has hurt you and try to gain some understanding about the situation.

- If you have ever been cheated, you may not be able to forgive and let go of your anger immediately. But try to think calmly through what happened and make sure you really do take the steps to protect yourself from something like this happening again. And then I would encourage you to try and gently release the anger, so that you can have peace of mind because just think how little you tend to accomplish when upset.

Buddha said that 'the way is in the heart'. A happy life is really a life that is full of love. When we allow ourselves to think, speak and act from our heart we become more generous, less grasping, more tolerant and patient of others and ourselves. We don't ignore the suffering of others but allow ourselves to feel it is ok to ask what we might be able to do, in whatever small way, to help. All of these things are aspects of the restful mind. We stop putting so much pressure on ourselves or others to be a certain way, we are more ready to laugh than scowl at the very same thing; a habit our partner has, a difficult situation. We stop holding on so tightly or running so fast and are able to once again simply sit for a while and maybe just listen to our partner's story of their day, not so impatient to tell our own. We remember how much we care about people in our lives; how lucky we are. We relax. Content.

Begin Today

I am always appreciative of the time people give to come to any teachings, and so I am very grateful to you for the time you are giving to read these words. It is a gift to me and I hope that you feel there are gifts in return from this book that you can take with you into daily life to encourage your restful mind. Giving and receiving teaching is perhaps even more precious than diamonds, as these are ideas that can be passed on or that you can use to benefit those around you.

If you practise, then you can transform your mind a little bit, and by transforming even a little you will be able to look at situations more calmly, no matter what. By understanding that happiness and suffering, beauty and ugliness, rich and poor are all perceptions in the mind, you will have a little more freedom in your life. With daily practice you can have the confidence not only to let go of anger or disappointment, but to truly live your life with compassion and generosity, to stop rushing around and be more present in the moment.

The effort that you have taken to read this book is like a spark in your mind; we say that all the teachings are about taking things step by step – and this is a great step. If you understand how your mind works, if you can tame your mind, it will give happiness, not only to you, but also to all your family and the people surrounding you. This is the kind of happiness that doesn't rely on any external conditions, but that comes from being at ease with your own mind. This happiness is only dependent on your own effort. It comes from within.

There are so many things that can give us the joy of living: a beautiful flower can give us the joy, a cup of coffee can give us the joy. The first step in developing a joyful life is to cultivate the sense of appreciation for life combined with the sense of impermanence, because if you don't have a sense of appreciation, then no matter how much you have you will always be thinking about what you want, what you wish to be next. And then we can have a sense of appreciation even without the beautiful flower or the cup of coffee. That is a great freedom.

To make a change is to be inspired. Don't be frightened to learn, to improve, because if you improve then you will have so much more to give. Make changes to how you think, speak and act readily and happily. Contemplate change and look at it from different angles. Think of how you try to change another person's mind through discussion – none of us wants to argue with a stone or a pillar. And so be flexible and open to yourself, as well as to others. Just as life is full of ups and downs, the same is true of your mind. And just as everything in life can change from one moment to the next, so too can you change your mind for the better.

It is with our minds that we create our world, so let us take care of and nourish our minds, rather than let them go wild and restless. We can bring peace and happiness into our minds whenever we wish, and we can give that peace and happiness to others through our love and kindness. By getting to know our minds beneath the loud and frenetic surface we get to know about life itself. We understand our need to connect with others, to be generous with others.

This is not something to make a big fuss about, it is a kind of life polishing as the life you have is already so precious and to be appreciated. But if you want to improve, then that is very good as it will open up your mind and give you the freedom you need to find your inspiration, your motivation and your happiness.

Never be complacent, keep checking in, keep searching for your own nature. Then relax, listen and dissolve. Your restful mind will be your friend for life.

Ten Simple Tools for the Restful Mind

1. See the good in life

You might not suddenly turn into someone who relentlessly sees the glass as half full after reading this book, and the world would be a very boring place if everyone were the same, but taking the time to notice what is going well in your life will nurture your restful mind, your patience, compassion and your happiness. Seeing the good in life, or being able to see things differently, can make you a more easy-going person and less quick to criticise both others and yourself. You won't compare yourself to others so much, will tend to be happier for others who do well and will simply appreciate life more.

2. Accept that life is full of ups and downs

To see the good in life is not to ignore the bad days or the challenges you face. But if you accept that life is something of a rollercoaster, then you also realise that everything is subject to change. And if everything is subject to change, then that must include your mind and your emotions too. You might get very angry about a situation, but instead of holding on to that anger for the whole day, week or beyond, so that it not only colours your day, but also your personality, you will find it easier to let it go, like a storm cloud in the sky or a wave crashing against the shore.

Acceptance is very freeing in that it allows you to focus on the things that you can change. Take the environment. It is very upsetting to many people that governments seem to do so little when it comes to taking better care of the environment. They feel helpless in that they can't hope to change these governments' ways. But if they focus instead on what they can do, they will understand that every single one of us can make a change, and so make a difference.

Acceptance isn't about giving up on things; it empowers you to see where to put your efforts, where best to focus your mind. And by accepting uncertainty we free ourselves from the weight of endless expectations and open ourselves up to the many rich and varied possibilities of life.

3. Come back into the present

The restless mind so often has its roots in a struggle with or against time. You panic about all the things you have to do today, or look further into the future and worry about what might happen. Will you get that promotion? What if you lose your job or become ill? Or you may think too much about what has already been and gone – about what you've said, the choices you've made, or why things can't be like they used to be.

Bring your mind back into the moment through all of your senses. What is happening right now? Children are so good at bringing us into the present; they aren't worried about tomorrow or wishing for yesterday. They're amazed by a train going by or catching a falling leaf. They are giggling at themselves and at us. They might be spared the responsibilities of adulthood, but they are a great reminder that joy is something you feel in the present moment, when you are caught up in the flow of doing a task well or eating a good meal. You can engage with the world, which increases your capacity to notice the suffering of others and care enough to do something – however small – about it.

Being more present also helps you to see rising emotions a little more clearly as they come, rather than being suddenly overwhelmed by them. You may feel the prick of embarrassment or annoyance, but because you are present you can look at it there and then and think: do I really need to be embarrassed or annoyed? Can I practise letting it go before it even has a chance to upset my peace of mind?

4. Love and being kind are what matters

The best part of developing a restful mind is that the capacity to give love and kindness grows. You have more space for others and begin to soften any hard edges to your attitudes, so that patience and tolerance move in where criticism and irritation once lived.

Material comfort and even wealth can be very

enjoyable, and striving to work hard and succeed in life is no bad thing at all. But beyond putting a roof over your head and food on the table, the balance in life will never come from material possessions. So if you can nurture your loving relationships and a more general love for humanity and the world, you will be going a long way towards bringing a feeling of balance to your mind.

Spend a little time each day within the Appreciation meditation (see p. 102) thinking about the love in your life and it will grow even more. Balance is so important in all aspects of life, that you should not be too strong in your attachments to anything. If you can give love with no conditions, then you can give it freely; you do not grasp at it. This is the kind of love that brings happiness to the restful mind. When you simply make others happy for no other reason than to bring them happiness, you feel very inspired by life.

Even if you have to criticise others in order to help them – say, as a boss, a teacher or a parent – you can do this with a sense of loving kindness. I think we all knew as children when instruction came from this place, and so even if we were hurt and upset on the surface, we felt deep down that we were learning something – we knew that what we were being told was for our own benefit.

We all know how it feels to experience the kindness of strangers; it touches our hearts. Be kind to strangers and to neighbours. Be kind to those closest to you. And the best way to do all of that is by being kind to yourself.

So if you can practise creating all of your thoughts, words and actions from a place of love within you, from your restful mind, then as well as helping others, you will also help yourself. To love others is to love yourself and to make a difference in others' lives is to have meaning in your own.

5. Sit

Don't be afraid of the quiet or of stillness. Sitting can be one of the hardest things for some people to begin with, but use your breathing techniques (see p. 89) and allow your body to relax into the moment. Give yourself a well-earned break. Don't worry if your thoughts run around your mind; as you sit, just imagine them gradually slowing down. See what is on your mind and let it just be. Sit on a bench once in a while and just feel the sun or the wind on your face. Sit by the fire and feel the warmth go through your body. Sit quietly at your desk before you switch on the computer (and always switch off your computer at the end of the day).

A few minutes of sitting will open up your whole day.

6. Do one thing at a time

How can we expect to be calm when we are doing three things at once? Why are we walking down the road and texting at the same time? Does busyness equate to happiness? Being a little more mindful in life means being able to focus on what truly matters and put your heart into all of your efforts. So if you are having a cup of tea, you can use those few minutes to relax and allow your mind to settle a bit. If you are working on a project, you can switch off the email and phone and immerse yourself in the task. If you are reading a story to your child you can be utterly present with them because you treasure time spent with them. And by doing one thing at a time you will tend to get more done, rather than constantly stopping and starting up again, wasting time getting back into a task that you had previously left off halfway through. Or you might even decide to do a few less things in the day, knowing that if just that one meeting or phone call goes very well, then you have had a good day, and that you don't need to cram busyness into every waking minute.

7. Laugh

What a great feeling it is when you can't stop laughing. Laughter lightens your load and lightens your step, bringing you right back into the moment. And it's the same with a smile. Both are ways in which to share happiness, to ease another person's upset or to diffuse a situation that could easily become tense. Laughter is also a great response to misunderstanding – rather than judge any differences, you can enjoy them.

It's good to see the funny side of things, and not take yourself too seriously. After all, we're all just human beings, doing our best.

8. Walk

To walk is to get back into the rhythm of the world and feel your own sense of balance in each step. When you walk you might remind yourself of your place in the world: that you are an individual and unique, but also that you are just one person among so many and that each and every one of us has both happiness and suffering in our lives.

Walking often has a way of providing perspective; you travel light and leave all your clutter behind, even for just a little while. You come back into your body, appreciating it and feeling each movement, waking yourself up. You might get back in touch with nature for this time, noticing the songs the birds sing or signs of the season. In the city you notice the signs of humanity in the people going by, and just as the seasons remind us of impermanence and change, so too do the buildings – some just being built, while others are beginning to fall down.

When you walk you naturally breathe more deeply, really getting the air into our lungs. You might contemplate emotions that have arisen during the day, looking at them calmly before letting them drift off. Or you might take this time to switch off and *just walk*.

9. Listen

It is good to get to know yourself through contemplation, but this is not to become self-centred or cut yourself off from the world and people around you. When the mind is restless you find it hard to settle enough to really listen to others. You are there in body, but your mind is elsewhere, thinking of a hundred different things. Or your opinions are so entrenched that you may offer up your view of the situation without trying to see things from the other person's perspective.

As you practise simply sitting and breathing, you become more used to being still and settled. And then you can really listen, which is an act of generosity not only to the speaker, but also to yourself, as you might learn something. Listen with an open mind and heart – you don't always need to offer solutions or answers, but as you listen with a restful mind, you become receptive and your wisdom or creativity might be sparked.

10. Embrace simplicity

Don't let things pile up, either around you or in your mind. If you allow situations or emotions to be stripped bare, then you begin to see them for what they are. You see anger for what it is – a fiery and strong emotion, but also one that you need not cling to. You begin to see complex decisions a little more clearly: you ask where is the greatest potential for generosity and happiness. What does the heart say? If I had no fear today, what would I do? You know you can't always control the outcome, but you sit more comfortably with yourself in the knowledge that each day you do your best.

Practise the art of letting go of things too, or taking care of what you already have rather than always looking for more. Just as your mind loves to have space in which to stretch and grow, your physical space has the same effect. You come into the world and leave with empty hands, so why spend quite so much time acquiring stuff in between?

You can practise simplicity in the way you eat: instead of filling your fridge with foods from all over the world that you might end up throwing away, you can be mindful of finding simple foods that have come from nearby. You really begin to appreciate the health-giving benefits of food, helping you to feel fit in body and energised in mind. You can slow down and take time over your meals, rather than always rushing to the next task. Remind yourself of the difference between what you want and what you need: what you need can be a very simple thing, while what you want can have no end.

End word

I realise that many people will worry about how to find the time to be restful and do all of the exercises in a book such as this one! But even if you were to practise the meditations I have introduced on just five days in a year, it will bring you five extra days of peace. If you can have a few days' holiday from your ego, I hope that sounds good. Spending a few minutes appreciating everything that you have, while realising the changing nature of life, will infuse your day. You will be more prepared for change, more flexible, more patient and, I think, happier. If it is a bad day, you will know that it won't last for ever. So I hope you will give these tools of the mind a go and see for yourself. More than that, I hope you will even change your life.

Recommended Reading

Walden: or Life in the Woods, Henry David Thoreau, Dover Publications, Inc., 1995 edition

Everyday Enlightenment, His Holiness Gyalwang Drukpa, Penguin, 2012

Thoughts Without a Thinker, Mark Epstein, Basic Books, 2004

The Tibetan Book of Living and Dying, Sogyal Rinpoche, Rider, 2008 edition

The Art of Happiness, His Holiness the Dalai Lama, Hodder Paperbacks, 1999

Why Kindness is Good For You, David R. Hamilton PhD, Hay House, 2010

Walking, Henry David Thoreau, available in various editions and online

books to help you live a good life

Join the conversation and tell
us how you live a #goodlife

🐦 @yellowkitebooks

📘 YellowKiteBooks

📌 Yellow Kite Books

📷 YellowKiteBooks